Monique Brynnel & Jon Weaving

MUSIC AND LOVE

Monique Brynnel & Jon Weaving

Music and Love

Monique Brynnel & Jon Weaving

with

Gillian Nikakis

First published in 2016

Copyright © Monique Brynnel & Gillian Nikakis 2016

All rights reserved. No part of this book may be reproduced or transmitted in any form or by any means, electronic or mechanical, including photocopying, recording or by any information storage and retrieval system, without prior permission in writing from the publisher. The Australian Copyright Act 1968 (the Act) allows a maximum of one chapter or 10% of this book, whichever is the greater, to be photocopied by any educational institution for its educational purposes provided that the educational institution (or body that administers it) has given a remuneration notice to Copyright Agency Limited (CAL) under the Act.

ISBN: 978-0-646-95027-3

A Cataloguing-in-Publication record is available from the National Library of Australia

Edited and produced by Ev Beissbarth

Further copies of this book can be purchased at:

www.bookstore.bookpod.com.au

This book is available as an e-book from most major on-line bookstores

Typesetting and cover design by BookPOD

Printed in Australia by BookPOD

www.bookpod.com.au

To our beloved son Jack.

Because of you all things became possible.

Let us go singing as far as we go: the road will be less tedious.
Virgil

Contents

Foreword *xiii*
Prelude *1*

Jon's Solo

Ljungskile, Sweden 4
Chapter One   Wonderful Melbourne, 1931 6
Chapter Two   The world of sound 10
Chapter Three   The ABC and Melbourne radio 19
Chapter Four   Singing studies in London, 1954 23
Chapter Five   'Ochee la hoolah, ochee la hey' 28
Chapter Six   London touring and Sadler's Wells 33
Chapter Seven   The beginnings of success 40
Chapter Eight   *Orpheus in the Underworld* 46
Chapter Nine   Touring Australia, 1962–66 50
Chapter Ten   Preparing for a European career 53
Chapter Eleven   Coda 64

Monique's Solo

Chapter One   The invisible tenor 71
Chapter Two   Gothenburg, 1940–48 74
Chapter Three   Alice and Styrbjörn Lindedal 84
Chapter Four   *My Fair Lady*... and off to London 95
Chapter Five   Money, money, money 98
Chapter Six   Back to Sweden 102
Chapter Seven   'Can't help loving that man of mine...' 107
Chapter Eight   'I can't give you anything but love...' 117
Chapter Nine   *Boeing Boeing*...and touring Europe 123
Chapter Ten   'I've found your Danilo!' 128

Duet

Chapter One	Kiel, 1969: the man with the voice	*135*
Chapter Two	The wedding	*143*
Chapter Three	*The Merry Widow*, Munich, 1970–78	*149*
Chapter Four	The honeymoon...eventually	*155*
Chapter Five	Australia	*163*
Chapter Six	Germany, 1971–74	*168*
Chapter Seven	Developments in Germany	*179*
Chapter Eight	To London again – and Jack!	*187*

Trio

Chapter One	A new beginning!	*195*
Chapter Two	Greta	*198*
Chapter Three	Fellini and surgery	*200*
Chapter Four	The *Ring*, everywhere	*204*
Chapter Five	The move to Sweden, 1976	*208*
Chapter Six	Life in Sweden	*210*
Chapter Seven	The deciding moment!	*225*

Finale   *230*
Acknowledgements   *234*
Singing technique   *233*
Select recordings   *242*
Index   *244*

Illustrations

Jon, aged about three, sitting on the moon   4
Jon with colleagues at 3UZ   14
Jon Weaving in his Sadler's Wells days   31
Before the transformation, Jon in *Orpheus in the Underworld*, London, 1960   48
Jon as Pluto, *Orpheus in the Underworld*, London, 1960   48
Jon as Hoffman in *Hoffman's Erzählungen*, Kiel, 1969   49
Australian tour of Sadler's Wells' production of *Orpheus in the Underworld*, Sydney, 1962   52
Ken Neate, Jon's cousin   58
Jon as Lohengrin, in *Lohengrin*, Kiel, 1968   61
Jon as Siegmund in *Die Walküre*, English National Opera, London, 1973–77   62
Jon as Siegfried in *Siegfried* with Rita Hunter, London, 1974   62
Jon as Bacchus in *Ariadne of Naxos*, English National Opera, London, 1973   65
Jon as Florestan in *Fidelio*, Cape Town, 1981   66
Brandtska Solist Familjen: Bertholdy, Bernhardina, Bernhard (aged three) with accompanying violinist at left, 1903   75
Monique, aged two   77
Erik Brynnel, at right, pictured with a friend, Gothenburg, 1935   80
Monique, aged 12, singing competition   85
Monique, aged 14, with Ken Lains' Orchestra, Gothenburg, 1953   86
The Merry Widow, Sydney, 1984, wearing Dame Joan Sutherland's hat!   90
Monique rehearsing *My Fair Lady* with Lauritz Falk, Gothenburg, 1961   95

Music and Love

Monique with Egon Larsson, *Lock Up Your Daughters*, Stockholm, 1962   *105*

Monique performing at Hamburger Bors in 1962   *106*

Monique as Magnolia in *Show Boat*, Stockholm, 1963   *109*

Monique in *Orpheus and Eurydice* with Rutger Nygren, Stockholm, 1966   *111*

Monique with Rutger Nygren and Erna Skaug, 1966   *111*

The cast of *Dial M for Murder*, Stockholm, 1967: seated, Lief Amble-Naess, Monique Brynnel; standing, left to right, Sten Gester, Roland Sandström, Ulf Lindquist   *112*

Show Boat, Stockholm, 1963, Monique as Magnolia, pictured with Rutger Nygren   *114*

Monique in *Die keusche Susanne*, Stockholm, 1966   *116*

Jazz concert in Leningrad, 1964   *120*

Boeing Boeing, Gothenburg, 1964: from left, standing: Karl-Arne Holmsten, Berndt Westerberg, Egon Larsson; seated Monique, Mona Åstrand and Solweig Lagström   *125*

Die Fledermaus, with Carrie Nielson, Stockholm, 1965   *126*

The Gypsy Princess, Baden bei Wien, 1968, with Josef Ebner (left) and Heinz Zednik   *129*

Jon and Monique, *The Merry Widow*, Kiel, 1969   *137*

Gertie, my friend and dresser   *139*

The first kiss in public, in *The Merry Widow*, Kiel, 1969   *139*

Jon in *Othello*, Kiel, 1969   *141*

Our engagement celebration dinner, cooked by Jon, 28 April 1969   *142*

The wedding day   *145*

Jon in *Faust*, Kiel, 1969   *147*

The Merry Widow, Munich, 1970   *151*

The Merry Widow, Munich, 1971   *152*

The Can Can dress   *154*

Belated honeymoon in Austria, 1970   *156*

The Count of Luxembourg, Kiel, 1970   *158*

Jon and Monique in the lead roles in *The Gypsy Baron*, Augsburg, 1971   *160*

Monique singing 'The Tipsy Song', *A Night in Venice*, Augsburg, c. 1972   *162*

ABC TV series, 'Monique & Jon', 1971   *167*

Jon and Monique in the lead roles, *Land of Smiles*, Augsburg, 1972   *169*

Jon as *Siegmund*, Leipzig, 1974   *173*

Jon as *Siegfried*, Leipzig, 1974   *174*

Jon as Siegmund in *Die Walküre*, London, 1974   *180*

The Gypsy Princess, Kiel, 1974   *187*

Monique with Nicholas Braithwaite, one day before Jack was born   *190*

Advertising poster showing Jon in *Siegfried*, London, 1976   *197*

Jon, with his mother Marg and son Jack, 1975   *207*

First winter in Sweden, 1976   *209*

Jack at Midsummer, Sweden, 1978   *212*

Das Feuerwerk, Bielefeld, 1975   *214*

Monique and Jon, *Show Boat*, Augsburg, 1972   *218*

Monique dressed for *The Gypsy Princess*, Gothenburg, 1977   *220*

Jon and Jack, England, 1977   *221*

The Gypsy Princess, Oslo, 1978   *224*

Alice and Styrbjörn Lindedal with Jon and Monique, Sweden, 1969   *227*

Monique as Adele in *Die Fledermaus*, Sydney, 1982   *230*

Nicholas Braithwaite (left), Richard Bonynge (centre) and Jon, Melbourne, 2008   *232*

Jon at the piano on New Year's Eve, Melbourne, 2010   *233*

Foreword

I first came across Jon Weaving when I saw him in Wendy Toye's famous and unforgettable, tastefully tasteless, production of *Orpheus in the Underworld* at Sadler's Wells – known to all and sundry as Orpheus in his Undershirt. I was coming towards the end of my student time and thanks to my father, a member of the conducting staff, was spending several evenings a week standing at the back of the Dress Circle at the Roseberry Avenue home of the company. Who could possibly forget this tall, handsome, commanding stage presence in his extraordinary and ridiculous purple costume!

I next met him when we were scheduled to perform the *Ring* together for Sadler's Wells Opera – by then the English National Opera – in 1974. The company had arranged a piano rehearsal for us as it was a first for me, and I think Jon's first Siegfried. I very quickly learnt the mettle of the man: after about 20 minutes of rehearsing, I made some point to him – undoubtedly a pearl of wisdom, of course – and Jon turned to the pianist and said, 'He's talking to me as if I were a tenor'. Ah. Jon was an ideal Siegfried. Tall, good-looking, a fine singer and a commanding stage presence – and altogether too intelligent for that stupid boy!

Jon was representative of that very talented group of Australians who 'made it' in London, and in European opera houses – Joan Hammond, Browning Mummery, Ken Neate, Glenda Raymond, Kevin Miller, Margaret Nisbett, Patricia Howard, June Bronhill, Ronald Dowd, Elizabeth Fretwell, Margreta Elkins, John Shaw and Marie Collier to name only a few. The most famous, of course, were Richard Bonynge and Dame Joan Sutherland. Jon himself notes that in the 1950s and 1960s the principal singers at Covent Garden and Sadler's Wells (later the English National Opera) were largely Australians, New Zealanders and Canadians – successful, he felt, partly because they had to work harder without local family and other support structures. It could be said that this really was the 'Golden Age' for expatriate Australian singers and the book reveals much interesting information about individual singers and productions of the time.

The snapshots of gloomy and damp boarding houses, appalling meals, chronic lack of funds, disastrous evenings in pubs, colleagues behaving badly and other aspects of touring truly illustrate the life of a musical nomad of the time. They will resonate with anyone who's ever gone on tour!

Monique refers in the book to the time when Jon was singing Siegmund in English for the English National Opera and in German in Germany, commuting between the two countries between performances. There is a line Siegmund sings in Act I, 'Kühlende Labung gab mir der Quell!' which, in the excellent Andrew Porter translation for the ENO, was 'Cool and refreshing'. Jon told me that one night he opened his mouth and went 'K' – or was it 'C'? – unable to remember which city he was in.

Both Jon and Monique describe the highs and lows of their careers through anecdotes interspersed with perceptive insights, and the book depicts with charm and honesty the joys and trials of their profession.

Jon and I became really good friends. An extremely intelligent man, with a sharp and very funny sense of humour (which could sometimes be misconstrued if people took it not in the spirit it was intended), I always found him to be a warm and generous man. At this time I had the great pleasure of meeting and getting to know his gorgeous wife, Monique, to the extent that I played squash with her the night before their son Jack was born. (If you believe that, you will believe anything, as will become apparent as you read the book!)

Foreword

As much social and musical history as autobiography, this book offers the reader the chance to travel on the musical journeys made by Jon and Monique, separately and together, at a time when it could be said that their art form was at its peak. It is an engaging and informative book that covers an era about which little has been written, and covers it entertainingly.

Quite coincidentally, my family and I moved to Australia in the 1980s much at the same time as Jon, Monique and Jack. As a result we were able to renew our friendship, and indeed to work together again. I was then Chief Conductor of the Tasmanian Symphony Orchestra and we did a couple of Viennese evenings there. They were superb. Jon acted as compère – though perhaps raconteur would be a better word – and the two of them gave our audience some of the most stylistically genuine Viennese music making I have heard, full of fun and of that special sentimentality that is peculiarly Viennese. This was the first time I had worked with Monique and discovered what a wonderful singer and stage animal she is: find 'The Tipsy Song' on YouTube, listen to her sing, and you will see what I mean. Utterly delightful.

And there was one evening in Hobart that in particular stays in my mind. We were at a restaurant and Jon – as usual – had us (and the whole of the restaurant) in stitches. At the same time Hinge and Brackett, a cross-dressing comedy duo who played a couple of genteel, slightly operatic spinsters, were in town doing their show. Towards the end of the evening one of the waitresses plucked up all her courage and came over to ask us, 'We know you are Hinge and Brackett but we want to know which is which.' So did we!

This is a greatly enjoyable book, detailing two extraordinary careers and a truly beautiful love story.

Nicholas Braithwaite

Prelude

My husband Jon was in his early seventies when he began writing about his life. After writing a few pages he allowed me to glance through what he had written, and selected some close friends to share the pages with. We were all enthralled and encouraged him to continue. After a few weeks, much to our disappointment, he stopped. Despite our nagging, he did not pick up the pen again until one day shortly before his death.

In the world of music there is a saying, 'If you can talk, you can sing'. In the world of literature perhaps it could be 'If you can hold a pen, you can write'. I have decided to finish what Jonny started. It is a daunting task, as I have never undertaken a writing project on this scale, and because it renews the sadness, the emptiness, and the grief.

The book is about our lives as two international singers, born worlds apart, one in Australia and one in Sweden. It is about how fate brought us together through a shared love of music and the human voice. It is also about not giving up, and about daring to approach new things.

I have included some advice and thoughts at the end of the book about how to prepare for a career as a professional performer. I believe that everyone can benefit both physically and psychologically from singing, whether professionally or for enjoyment.

Singing can be a difficult career to follow, but also an incredibly rewarding one. The boundless joy that his art brought to Jon and to his audiences, and the joy that singing continues to bring to me, is a privilege to experience. This book is about music, love and dreams coming true.

Jon's Solo

Ljungskile, Sweden

April to September 2011

I have just been told that, in all probability, I have an incurable illness. This has inspired me to return to the keyboard, so that the extraordinary story of my life is recorded.

Jon, aged about three, sitting on the moon

Many names will be changed to protect the guilty, but some will remain unaltered. There does not seem to be a point in telling a story about a famous conductor, if the reader does not know about whom I am writing. Many of the stories have passed into legend in the musical world, and are apocryphal. Some events seem just too good to have actually happened so I intend to keep them alive and well.

My mother always said that she had the feeling at my birth that I might become a singer. At the end of her long labour, at ten to five in the afternoon of 23 February 1931, a nurse entered the room and announced that she had just heard on the radio that Dame Nellie Melba had died. As if in sympathy, I cried as I entered the world. The nurse felt this was an omen and immediately said, 'Obviously he is going to be a singer!'

Chapter One

One is always at home in one's past.
Vladimir Nabokov

Wonderful Melbourne, 1931

The thought comes home to me every day that being born in Australia in the 1930s gave me the opportunity to enjoy Australia at its best. I feel sad for my son Jack, as the quality of innocence evident in those times has gone. I'm sure Jack thinks he has a great life, having a secure background and parents who love him, but he has no experience of the innocence that I remember.

My childhood home was in Auburn Road, Hawthorn. I was an unhealthy child on a strict diet. My mother banned stone fruit; in fact she allowed no fruit at all that had not been boiled or stewed. If she only knew! There were all sorts of fruit trees in the garden and I hid amongst them and stuffed myself full of figs, apricots, plums and peaches.

As children, we enjoyed a freedom that would be unthinkable today. The family had a beach house on the Mornington Peninsula. On holiday mornings, my grandfather and I walked from Fisherman's Beach in Mornington, carrying our buckets, across paddocks and the Nepean Highway to Sonnenberg's farm, where we collected the milk, fresh from the cow. Now there are so many choices of milk in the supermarket it's hard to know where to start and those paddocks are suburban blocks.

In my childhood, summer used to start on 1 November, but now summer commences in earnest at the beginning of January. During the school holidays my family spent from November onwards at the beach, where we gently basted ourselves with coconut oil, and slowly acquired a tan so we felt and looked wonderfully healthy at the end of summer.

Every morning I walked to my school in Rathmines Road, and every day I went home for lunch. At recess I joined in whatever was currently in vogue which could have been marbles, spinning tops, or a game called 'British Bulldog'. On Monday, everyone turned up as if by magic with marbles, then a few weeks later it would be something quite different. Somehow everyone except me knew about the new trend. Even when I did know, and brought my marbles to school, I had usually lost the lot by the end of the first recess. This was because there was one particularly unfair custom I remember, called 'grab dates when the bell goes'. This was the cue to scrimmage, pillage and plunder.

Across the road, on the corner of Fletcher Street, lived a family of Plymouth Brethren. Having no brother or sister, I was fortunate to be taken in by the children and made part of their family. Their back garden had a gate opening on to a tennis court that belonged to a local church, and we made full use of the space.

Australia suffered large outbreaks of polio in the 1930s and, because of the fear of contagion, our school was closed for a short period. I felt I was in heaven. An English woman, Jean Lawson, established an educational program on Radio 3DB and my friends and I sat on the floor in front of the radio where we supposedly carried on with our education. It was a token gesture, and we were soon back outside on the tennis court.

Next door was a property with a huge back garden, where large trees crowded together and the undergrowth was tall enough to hide in. It felt like a mysterious jungle to a young boy and in all the time we lived next door I never saw a person at the property. On the other side of this mystical place lived a girl from school whose parents had a mulberry tree. It was fashionable to keep silkworms but useless trying to keep them without access to mulberry leaves, so the mulberry tree next door was indeed a treasure. I can still smell them now and hear the rustling in the shoebox by my bed, as the thick white caterpillars crawled around and over the twigs and foliage. It's difficult to believe now that we used to put the cocoons in our mouths, pull out a thread of silk and spin it onto a homemade frame. I never managed to make more than the occasional bookmark, but the sensation was wonderful. There was sadness, too, when the time came to release the emerging moths.

Another advantage to climbing the mulberry tree was that we could look into the jungle next door and try to see a house or a person. There was a glimpse of a grey slate roof, but nothing more. I did hear that the owner was a Mrs Gregory, but she might as well have been a ghost.

Another neighbor, Mrs Gibb, used to prophesy from the Bible and would frequently fill our ears with frightening prognostications. She told my parents about the Second World War, long before it happened.

Although my childhood memories are of a freedom perhaps not experienced by the youth of today, there was another side to the Australia I grew up in.

Before the outbreak of World War II was a parochial, isolated and unsophisticated country that considered itself an extension of the 'mother' country. It was aware – and a little ashamed – of its convict history.

Melbourne is Australia's second-largest city but it was a dull place for overseas visitors. One celebrity described it as a 'cemetery with lights'. Ava Gardner, who starred in *On the Beach*, a film made in Melbourne about the end of the world, reportedly commented that

Melbourne was 'the perfect place to make a film about the end of the world'. Pubs and hotels were forbidden to sell alcohol after 6.00 p.m. and this meant the streets were deserted as people chose to drink at home or in hidden areas to evade law enforcement.

The innocence and somnolence of 1960s Melbourne was matched by its security and tranquility. It was a time of increasing prosperity, and new opportunities.

Chapter Two

Singing is in fact sustained speech.

The world of sound

From the earliest time I can remember, I was in love with the human voice. I am sometimes asked to be an adjudicator for vocal competitions and I find that, even with the worst and the most hopelessly untalented singer performing, there is magic and communication in someone singing to me.

It all began with a chance event, one that delivered both a shock and great delight. When I was about four years old, my mother and I were walking along Collins Street in Melbourne, after lunch at the Russell Collins teahouse, when we passed the Regent Theatre. Suddenly my mother asked if I would like to go to the pictures. I still remember my surprised realization that an event would go on whether I attended it or not. For the first time I had a sense of a world outside my own childish self-absorption.

The film was *One Night of Love* with Grace Moore, the American soprano who was later killed in a plane crash. From then on, my fate was sealed and I have never lost the thrill, the magic and enchantment of hearing a wonderful voice.

In the sixty years I have been attending operatic performances all over the world, perhaps twenty of those years have been truly memorable and an unalloyed joy. The greatest singers are only human and can have 'off nights'. The casting can be uneven, a diva surrounded by artists of lesser talent, or there can be just one chorus member whose eyes are wandering away from what is happening. The spell is broken.

I feel completely let down when, on entering an opera house, I find the curtain already open, stage hands smoking cigarettes while wandering around setting up scenery and props, and the stage manager holding a plastic cup of coffee.

The magic of the proscenium between the audience and the stage, the curtain opening after the overture, revealing a world into which one must enter with complete belief, is to me one of the great joys of the theatre.

Opera audiences of all ages must retain and maintain the sense of childish wonder and participation that is intended, by brilliant composers, brilliant stage directors and years of preparation. This is all too often destroyed when young directors attempt to explain and interpret what the composer and librettist really meant. In the process in many cases the original essence – the magic – is lost.

I have had the great good fortune in the last sixty years to hear most of the great voices in person. I seem to have an indelible memory for voices and timbre, and I have been able to retain the sound so that I can pass on to my students, with certainty, what is good, and what is mediocre. I was totally in love with singing and, thank goodness, my parents were also interested enough to give me the opportunity to hear everyone and everything that was going on in Melbourne.

For a small country like Australia, it is sometimes hard to believe that we hold such a respected and significant place on the international stage when it comes to the world of opera. It was a series of colourful characters, talented singers and visionary organizations that helped to put us there. Much credit needs to go to Dame Nellie Melba who achieved legendary status during her lifetime. She was the operatic world's most famous diva during her career of almost four decades. Australia should be grateful to J. C. Williamson who brought large productions, and large theatres to stage them in, to Australian audiences. He died in 1913 and the Tait brothers took charge of the company. They began to bring visiting artists to Australia, including the Russian dancer Anna Pavlova and her company, the Ballets Russes, followed by the Bolshoi Ballet company and the Borovansky company as well as many other large dance companies.

J. C. Williamson provided a regular source of employment for Australian dancers, singers and actors throughout the 1940s, 1950s and 1960s. The company presented musicals such as *Annie Get Your Gun, Oklahoma, Brigadoon, Kiss Me Kate, South Pacific, The Pyjama Game* and *My Fair Lady*. There were concerts at the Melbourne Town Hall, and nights at what was then His Majesty's Theatre to hear Gladys Moncrieff in *The Maid of the Mountains*, Fred Murray in *White Horse Inn* and every single performance of the visiting Gilbert and Sullivan Company. The names of the singers are burnt into my brain to this day – Ruby Riddell, Gregory Stroud, Ivan Menzies, John Clements, Eva Blair, and Max Oldaker. Even now, without ever having sat down to learn them, I can still sing all the songs.

This stood me in good stead for my first step onto the stage at the Hawthorn Town Hall, where I sang the Pirate King in a school production of *Pirates of Penzance*. It was a great debut. On the second line in my opening song, my faithful Samuel was to throw a large skull-and-crossbones flag for me to catch.

'Oh, better by far to live and die...' when, WHACK! He threw it one line too early, caught me on the side of the head, and down I went.

I was able to use this episode when I directed *The Pirates of Penzance* at Her Majesty's Theatre in Auckland in the 1960s, but at the Hawthorn Town Hall the valuable experience fell on deaf and ringing ears.

During my primary school years I had dreamed of attending Melbourne High School, so you can imagine my feelings after so many years of breathless planning, when I was expelled after half an hour. During the World War II the school was requisitioned by the American military. This happened just as I was to start my time at the school. I was sent to a new school that had opened near home, Camberwell High School. This was an all-boys school committed to Christian values. The hymns sung in chapel were based on English composers and perhaps influenced my music appreciation initially.

There was an English teacher there to whom I am eternally grateful. He instilled in me a love of the spoken word as he rolled words off his tongue with a relish and a precision that made a huge impression, long before I discovered that singing was in fact sustained speech. If you don't enunciate well, don't bother to sing: there is nothing worth sustaining.

Apart from the English lessons and the great poetry, I hated school. Although I was good at everything, I felt I was wasting my time as my life was going to be about music and I wanted to get on with it. I had the great luck to meet Jessey Schmidt, and began taking singing lessons with her. By today's standards, the lessons were a joke. There were always at least seven or eight students there for every lesson, and people kept dropping in to sing some 'naws'.

Jessey could only play two exercises, one of which was *Brahms' Lullaby* and she sang only 'naw' to the melody. Everyone took turns at doing this over her yells to 'lift your bloody support'. Occasionally, when persuaded, she would accompany herself in Massenet's *Élégie*, a cigarette hanging out of her mouth and one eye closed against the smoke. Her breath control was wonderful. She passed this knowledge of support for the voice to countless hopefuls, many of whom progressed to international careers.

One of these was Lance Ingram, who went on from the Galleon Coffee Lounge in St Kilda to being first tenor of the Paris Opera. He has also been referred to as Australia's greatest ever tenor and was certainly one of the leading French tenors. If you have seen the film of *Tosca* with Maria Callas, the tenor is Lance, although he is acknowledged as 'Albert Lance'. The French thought that 'Ingram' sounded like a sneeze and insisted on a change. Thanks to the famed French voice teacher Dominic Modesti virtually locking him up in an attic with an old seamstress, Lance learned to speak perfect French. However, this never changed him and his Aussie ways. One day when I was living in Paris, I was walking along Rue Lepic when I heard an unmistakably 'ocker' male voice:

'Bloody Weaving!'

And there he was, as large as life, on the other side of the road. He was very much the figure of the successful operatic tenor, but lovable and, in manner, as simple as ever.

Jon with colleagues at 3UZ

Feeling that school was of no benefit to me, I begged my parents to let me leave. This was no small thing in those days. To leave half-way through Intermediate Certificate (year 8) was a huge step, but Jessey Schmidt knew Mr Prince, the manager of 3UZ, one of Melbourne's many commercial radio stations. He gave me a job in the record department. I thought I had died and gone to heaven.

All radio stations at that time played a mix of music, and 3UZ devoted a great deal of time to classical programs – hard to imagine now, but true. Of course, the records we played were all 78s. We had to run up to 3XY or 3DB to borrow the identical copies of a symphony, for instance, to enable us to crossfade from one disc to another instead of having to pause while turning the record over.

The announcers at 3UZ were interesting characters. One of the weirdest was Gil Charlesworth who ran the afternoon program from two until five, when Tiny Snell, an enormous man, took over for *Hello the Hospitals*. I was really green – wet behind the ears – and had never heard of a 'cough button'. This was the little button you could press to cut the microphone momentarily, without interfering with the red light glowing that told people you were on the air, live.

Gil started off his program every day with a book reading. With his headphones on, he crouched forward and crooned into the microphone. I knew from his mail that there were hundreds of swooning ladies hanging on every word! It was shortly after my first day at work there, and I crept into the studio while the red light was on. I was carrying a huge, heavy pile of records, the listener's requests for *Hello the Hospitals*. I was to leave these for Tiny Snell's operator.

'Gilbert the Filbert', as he was known, was just coming to the end of that day's episode in the novel.

'And so we leave Lady So and So and Lord So and So in the summer house. ...What are they doing?'

Unknown to me, he hit the cough button, then said, 'Why, they're having a fuck!'

My heart lurched and I dropped the whole pile of records, which smashed to smithereens. It was shortly after the war so most of them were irreplaceable. Heaven help the requests for the hospitalized, most of whom were our armed forces personnel. Gil didn't turn a hair and went on without a hint of a break. 'Listen in tomorrow at the same time for the next episode.'

I headed for the toilet, very quickly.

As microphones treated my speaking voice very well and I was desperately ambitious, I was on air in six months as a full-blown announcer, the youngest in Melbourne. My record boy, who used to get a pie for me for lunch, was Graham Kennedy.

A pie for lunch! To this day, if you walk along Bourke Street from the Windsor Hotel and come to the first lane, you can see through coats of whitewash the image of a huge tree – the sidewall of the Cedar of Lebanon café. This business specialized in homemade pies and in fact had a pile of them lying in the right-hand shop window, a spot that usually caught all the available sunshine. This is probably why a large Persian cat that basked there every day surmounted the pile of pies. On entering and ordering a pie, the huge and somewhat greasy-looking owner shoved the cat out of the way, grabbed a pie, held it up, and carefully blew all the fur off it before handing it to you.

My direct boss, Johnny McMahon, went on holidays and Norman Ellis and I were left in charge of presenting his show *Christie's Radio Auditions*, for two weeks. In the days before television this was a very important program. Anyone could write in for a chance to air their talent, hoping for a one-, two-, or even three-gong award. People wrote in weeks in advance to get seats to see the show 'live' in the 3UZ auditorium in Bourke Street.

Act one. A tall lady walked up to the microphone and announced that she was going to do bird imitations. She said she was very nervous and asked if she could have a glass of water. The kitchen was a floor below the studio, and well locked at this time of night. Someone hurried downstairs to get her a drink while I filled in, live to air, with whatever drivel I could think of. Finally the water arrived, and she took a mouthful. She let out a most enormous gulp and said, 'That's a swallow!', bowed to the audience and walked off.

I was young, if that is an excuse, and I started to get the giggles.

One gong!

The next act was a man who held a music box up to the microphone and allowed it to tinkle out a barely recognizable tune.

One gong!

The trouble was that he couldn't stop it, despite desperately pushing matches into various parts of the poor instrument's anatomy. It played through the next three acts, supplying a very discordant accompaniment. By now I was displaying traces of hysteria, as each act was worse than the one before. I barely got through the night.

The next day, the manager, Lew Bennett, called me in to his office and offered me the sack or the chance to go on the morning program with Nicky. Cliff Nicholls (alias Nicky) was a famous radio personality, a man I had run home from school to listen to when he presented the children's program on 3AW.

Nicky was to join 3UZ, and was considered a huge catch. My nose was properly out of joint, but I made the most of it and actually had a lot of fun in the three months I lasted with Nicky. He was a very funny man and we managed to clown our way through many of the programs. We sang duets from *Il Trovatore*, invaded the cooking program on toy scooters, and insulted all the major advertisers who, after the initial shock, just loved it.

Every morning there was the standard announcement: 'It's ten o'clock and the Commonwealth Bank is now open for business.'

It was Nick's first morning and he spotted the effects cabinet in the corner of the studio. It was a large box on wheels and every side of the box had a door. Each door had numerous types of locks, bolts, rasps, padlocks, squeaky hinges and so on – everything that might be needed for a radio play. We wheeled this over to the mike and at precisely ten o'clock we started: 'It's ten o'clock...'. Then followed seven minutes of rattling, banging, hammering, dropping lengths of chain and opening locks at least fifty times. Finally, after great gasps and groans of exhaustion, Nick said:

'The bloody bank is finally open for business.'

It's hard to credit this today, but this caused a riot somewhat like a minor Orson Welles Martian episode. The switchboard was flooded with calls, praise and protests mixed fairly evenly. Such strong reaction was strange, considering that over my years at 3UZ, the 'F' word went out on air about five times and there was never a whisper from the listeners. Perhaps no one would admit hearing it, let alone recognizing it.

My nose was still a bit out of joint and so I arranged to do an audition for the ABC for the job of general announcer, temporary bottom class.

Chapter Three

Good music is very close to primitive language.

The ABC and Melbourne radio

My ABC audition took place one afternoon at Broadcast House which was opposite the Law Courts on the corner of Lonsdale and William Streets in Melbourne. I was met in the foyer by Norman Blee, a charming man who later became a firm friend. Norman Blee was a well-known ABC voice and personality, and he made me feel at home. I was given a script to read which contained some news and then a lot of classical music to introduce in German, Italian and French. I got through it all fairly well and Norman came into the studio to show me out.

'Well, your German needs bit of work, otherwise, very good', he said encouragingly, and off I went. When I got home to Canterbury there was a telegram offering me the job waiting for me. The telegram was from Geoff Norton, and I received a following letter from him setting out conditions, hours and salary and asking me to start as soon as possible. I don't remember giving notice at 3UZ or any of the departure from 45 Bourke Street, but it was not a sad time as I knew I would keep in touch with all my friends. This proved to be true, and fifty-five years later we still meet for a laugh.

My departure left the door open for Graham Kennedy who, after a short break when others were auditioned, took over my position with Nicky, and was sitting in the box seat when television began in Australia in 1956.

Graham went on to become known as the King of Television and was a living legend. He died in 2005 and the consensus of opinion is that he will never be replaced. He ended his years almost as a recluse, living in the Southern Tablelands of New South Wales at Canyonleigh, where he bred his beloved horses.

The day arrived for me to commence at the ABC and I met Geoff Norton and Harold Rosenthal, the studio supervisor. The first question they asked was, 'You *are* over twenty-one, aren't you?'

There I was with a salary offer in my hand, and they were just finding out that I was a junior, and by ABC standards entitled only to a weekly wage lower than I had been receiving at 3UZ. Naturally, I protested strongly but their hands were tied – as were mine. I had burnt my bridges and had to accept the conditions despite my muttered murmurings about suing and false pretences. Eventually they did manage to make it up to me financially and I settled in to one of the happiest times of my life.

The announcing staff was made up of old BBC men, young ex-servicemen, naval officers and a few 'normal' eccentric locals. Everyone was a character and absolutely fascinating. Tom Horeton was a brilliant pianist on the side. His friend Kevin McBeath ran a new music society and his father owned Thomas Music, the best record shop in Melbourne. Laidley Mort, an actor, was just leaving under some sort of cloud. There were other personalities like Eric Coleman, brother of famous film star Ronald Coleman, and two alcoholics, who I was told were never to be allowed near a microphone. Jim Tregonning was also leaving for 3AW. His major crime, at the end of a small run of misdemeanours, was when he announced Brahms' *Pastoral Symphony* one morning in the symphony hour. The switchboard ran hot with people indignantly phoning in. At the conclusion of the Symphony, Jim opened the mike.

'That was Beethoven's *Pastoral Symphony* and I would like to thank the people who took the trouble to leave their radio sets, went to the telephone and phoned about this trifling mistake. However, whilst you were away you missed some very, very fine music!'

Not ABC standards. This was a time when everyone spoke in an almost BBC accent, and some programmes required the announcer to wear full evening dress. It was a time when radio was supreme. The ABC was the most supreme.

At 3UZ, I had been spoilt. Everyone had a turntable operator, but at the ABC I not only had to set up my own records but also – since it is a national broadcaster – be ready to switch to Sydney at preset times for interstate programmes. The Postmaster General's staff supposedly handled all the technical stuff, such as switching, levels, and studio changes. The PMG boys were the power behind the throne and, unless they were out of their control booths and upstairs playing table tennis, they managed to do their duties. They were generally a great lot of guys and made my time at the ABC very happy indeed.

It is hard today to imagine Melbourne in the late 1940s and early 1950s. Foreign food was practically unknown. One day I was taken out to lunch by Eric Hambley, the Head of the Record Library, to a restaurant in Exhibition Street. He ordered spaghetti bolognese for us both. I had never been exposed to such a delicious aroma. A difficulty arose when I realized I had no idea how to get the food into my mouth and, despite my host's encouragement, sat there literally drooling and unable to taste the wonderful concoction. The sheer frustration is a vivid memory.

Wonder of wonders, a Chinese restaurant opened almost next door to the studios and this is something else that lingers in my gastronomic memory. The first taste of a spring roll was magical. This was a real hand-made delicacy stuffed with prawns, pork, cabbage, spring onions and heaven knows what else, to produce a luscious start to the meal. Oddly enough, although I ate there dozens of times, the only main course I can remember is chop suey. Arthur, the owner and chef, made cabbage unforgettable. Even allowing for the virgin state of my taste buds, I have rarely experienced such wonderful enjoyment of Asian food and I have since eaten in all parts of the world.

Of course there were more marvellous restaurants: Florentino, Mario's and the Oriental Hotel to mention just three, but they were expensive at that time despite the prices being somewhat south of ludicrous by today's standards. Wine lists were a joke. Mind you, in some places drinking is still an adventure.

Only a few years ago, my wife Monique and I were in Goondiwindi on the New South Wales and Queensland border. We asked in the hotel dining room for a wine list (this produced a snigger from the waitress). I was directed to the bottle shop. This turned out to be a serving hatch in the lane beside the hotel. After knocking, the flap finally opened to reveal the same waitress. In answer to my question, 'What white wine do you have?', the reply was, 'We only have Riesling or Riesling.'

Chapter Four

Sing exercises with an easy medium volume.
Blasting only helps miners.

Singing studies in London, 1954

It was the fashion in the 1940s and 1950s to aim to study abroad with the famous Italian lyric tenor, Dino Borgioli. He had become the director of vocal studies at the New Opera Company of London. Prior to this the popular teacher was Dingh Gilly, an Algerian. He was a stylish, intelligent singer who taught the Australian operatic baritone John Brownlee and, earlier still, taught Mathilda Marchesi who went on to teach Emma Calve and Nellie Melba.

In 1952 Margaret Nisbett, an Australian soprano, and I married, and in 1954 we came to London. Margaret had won the Mobil Quest, and the prize included the chance to study in Europe. Our first thought was to contact Signor Borgioli and audition for him, in the hope of becoming his students (he had taught an earlier winner of the Quest, Joan Sutherland). Our son Jon was born in 1955.

Borgioli had been interned in England during the war and had emerged into London's civilian life to form the Cambridge Opera Company. He brought famous and mature artists such as the Italian baritone Mariano Stabile to London to sing in *Don Pasquale*, and engaged emerging local singers, such as the Welsh baritone Martin Lawrence, to produce highly successful productions that delighted opera-starved London audiences. He was married to an Australian, Patricia Mort. They lived in a studio in Holland Park owned by Eric Aitken, an enthusiastic amateur operatic tenor. There were many Australians studying with Dino and I particularly remember Patricia Howard and the Australian coloratura soprano Glenda Raymond.

Before Glenda Raymond's time in London, Hector Crawford (known as the 'father-to-be' of Australian television) persuaded her to star in a radio serial in the 1940s. This was 'The Melba Story' which comprised 78 half-hour episodes. Hector, with the assistance of soprano Pauline Bindley, coached Glenda through the extraordinary range of Melba's repertoire.

When she returned to Melbourne in 1950, Glenda accepted Hector's proposal of marriage and they formed a wonderful partnership. Years later, Crawford was to comment, 'She would have had a career that was miles better than mine if she'd stayed in London – she's a much bigger talent than me.'

Dino's accompanist was a most famous lady, Madame Adami (Poppy) whose name appeared on record labels at the beginning of recording history, playing for legendary singers such as Anton Van Rooy.

Poppy adopted us at once and was always a tower of strength and encouragement. We also hit it off with Dino and saw quite a bit of him socially as well as working regularly in his studio. He was a real character and had a wealth of theatrical stories. He was also a proud and aggressive Italian. He took me several times to Chez Ciccio's Restaurant in Church Street, Kensington. Ciccio was a great friend who had been interned with Dino, and no menu was ever offered. Food just appeared at the table.

Another regular at the restaurant was Princess Margaret and I remember her complaining (quite rightly, too) about the objectionable odour of Dino's cheroots interfering with her meal. The Princess was offered another table – not us!

There were many nights when I was invited to stay back and share a glass of wine with Dino in the studio. Then out came the records and I was able to record his singing and his compositions from original 78s. The recording was possible as I had managed to purchase a Grundig tape recorder. Although tape was an almost unaffordable luxury for us, I copied everything of Dino that was offered. I have these recordings to this day. I also have a rare copy of the two of us singing the duet from *La Bohème*. He permitted me to be the tenor and he took the baritone part. I also have a recording of an interview and recital of Tuscan songs recorded live on the BBC one afternoon in 1955. He accompanied himself on the piano and although sometimes sounding a little old, the unmistakable timbre and style were still very evident.

He was teaching Herbert Lom and Valerie Hobson at this time. They were appearing in *The King and I* at Drury Lane. Dino asked me to help him in a lesson with Herbert. I was demonstrating and explaining several points whilst my faithful Grundig captured the results, when Herbert Lom suddenly swung around and knocked the recorder off the piano. The fragile plastic case shattered on the parquet floor and I knelt to collect the bits and assess the damage.

'Don't worry, I will pay!' said the famous King of Siam.

'No, don't think about it,' said the proud and completely impoverished singer from Melbourne.

'Well, that's very decent of you,' said Lom, and there the matter rested.

Had he but known, we were on the point of starving! The little money I had was jealously saved for lessons. I had taken a job with a stationery company and was 'cold calling' in the City of London selling carbon paper, typewriter ribbons and envelopes. My salary was £5 a week, and another pound in expenses. The rent for the Gloucester Road basement bedsitter was four guineas!

Borgioli agreed with the Australian opinions about my voice being really a tenor and all our work was concentrated on retraining my technique to enable me to sustain the higher tessitura. This was quite funny, as the Italian version of my name is Giovanni Tessitura and many people will know that the tessitura of a song or a role is the general area where it lies vocally. Many baritones, Peter Dawson included, could sing a high C but could not possibly sustain the tessitura of an operatic aria through to the end.

Browning Mummery, the lauded Australian tenor, well known to the general public as Rudolfo in *La Bohème* to Melba's Mimi in the farewell performance at Covent Garden, was recorded for posterity by HMV. He used to say that I had a bastard voice. It could have been anything between bass baritone and tenor. Only time would tell. Well, time was telling and it was progressing quite well except for one small thing. I mentioned earlier the tenor Eric Aitken. He and Dino had formed an Operatic Concert Company so they could perform together.

Signor Aitken was to sing the lead tenor roles, performing bleeding operatic chunks. I was engaged along with June Bronhill and Len Weir to perform with him in venues such as the Bexhill Pavilion and the Concert Hall in Eastbourne.

We were transported to the performances in a magnificent old Rolls Royce and, I can tell you, the performances and the subsequent fees were keenly sought after. The only problem was that despite Dino training me as a tenor, I was appearing in his concerts singing baritone roles such as Germont père, Rigoletto, Valentine and Rossini's Figaro. It was a musical see-saw. It was obvious that there was a dilemma when one day, on his return from lunch with the head of BBC television music, Dino calmly told me that Sir Thomas Beecham was to conduct a TV performance of *Barber of Seville* and I was to sing the baritone role of Figaro. He went on to mention that he had made himself personally responsible for my Italian so there was nothing to worry about – just the fact that I would have been much happier singing the tenor role of the count!

Len Weir and I had always regarded each other as family, thanks to the close friendship of an aunt of his with an uncle of mine. We played cricket together for Australia House where I opened the bowling and he the batting against some interesting teams. The grounds were beautiful but I had never played on a turf wicket before. Joining the Australia House team was a wonderful experience and it was a privilege to watch some of my team mates at the wicket. Some of them were sub-district players in Australia and their talent won us a lot of matches.

Len and his wife Beverly lived a bohemian life above an onion store in Covent Garden, while he, like us, tried to make his mark. He had a lovely lyric tenor and his duets with June Bronhill were always a highlight of our concerts, so much so that Eric Aitken stopped appearing and Len became the sole tenor in the group.

Chapter Five

*Singing benefits. The brain produces endorphins,
a natural antidepressant and painkiller.*

'Ochee la hoolah, ochee la hey'

Rutland Boughton's opera *Bethlehem* was getting one of its rare performances at the Kingsway Town Hall, a well-known venue for slightly weird and wonderful works, and my friend Tom Swift had been given a lead role in this largely amateur production. Tom had recently joined the group after his rather hasty and unplanned exit from the chorus of *Kismet* at Drury Lane. Unfortunately, Tom's vocal prowess was unable to save him when he forgot himself after several large beers and vomited into Doretta Morrow's dress which was lying open on the floor of the wings ready for her to step into for a quick change. It was evident that the crinoline was unable to hold both the delicious Miss Morrow and the contents of Tom's lunch, liquid and otherwise, and he was sacked on the spot. Vocally, it was musical theatre's loss and opera's gain.

Tom's chance to prove himself as a serious operatic talent was here in *Bethlehem*. He had been given the solo role of the coal-black king, one that requires the clever concealment of pasty white skin in order to be believable. Who could forget the darkened Tom advancing down the stage, arms held high, hands gesticulating madly while singing the immortal words 'Ochee la hoolah, ochee la hey', when he suddenly stopped and exclaimed to the assembled cast and at the very least the front three rows of the stalls, 'Oh Jesus Christ, I forgot to make up my hands!' He made an attempt to hide them behind his back and carried on, but his singing was drowned out somewhat by the hilarity on stage, in the orchestra and throughout the audience.

It was through Sadler's Wells Opera Company chorus that I became involved in this sparkling production. An urgent call for help had gone out to Sadler's Wells for vocal assistance, with volunteers being called for from the chorus, particularly for two tenors who could read music (a somewhat arduous task for many tenors). Arthur Thelwell and I offered our services and discovered quickly why reading music was such an integral part of the appointment. Our first look at the music was on opening night. We were handed horse-blanket ponchos to slip on over our street clothes, given rather enormous bright orange-coloured music scores, and told to crouch down behind the chorus and sing as loudly as possible.

Onto the stage we crept and did our best with the unfamiliar music, hunched down on bent knees at the back of the choir. We came to the end of the first chorus, and I fumbled with my score, and attempted to turn the page to see what came next. It's hard to say who was more startled, the audience or me, when I looked up to find that the barefoot cast had parted neatly in the middle and silently departed the stage. They left behind a hunched-up man, clutching a large bright orange score, wearing a horse-blanket with trousers and lace-up leather shoes. I vaguely remember drawing myself upright, tucking my orange score under my wing, bowing, and getting off the stage with as much dignity as the hoots and howls would allow. The performance was all downhill from there. However, the night's shining light of hilarity and artistic, interpretative brilliance forever belongs to the veteran soprano singing the Virgin Mary who, bless the old dear, appeared on stage looking like the Virgin Mary's grandmother.

Music and Love

Staggeringly, the evening was counted as a success and a further performance was arranged in the composer's hometown of Glastonbury. Mercifully, the performance was much improved. Tom retained his role and this time I exited with the rest of the cast. The dim lighting hid a multitude of faults, including the rapidly aging Virgin Mary.

After the performance Tom was starving, as usual, and somehow managed to find two meat pies smothered in sauce and wrapped in newspaper. We settled into the back seats of the bus returning to London and, as it drew away from the scene of triumph, Tom took his first mighty bite of what turned out to be a thoroughly rancid pie. Without thinking, and with his normal spontaneity, Tom attempted to throw it out of the window. Unfortunately, as the window was a row ahead of us Tom failed to notice that it was shut – not that it mattered anyway, as he missed completely, and managed to hit the man sitting on the aisle in front of us just behind his right ear. When the victim turned, I noticed with dismay that he was in fact an extremely famous and well-dressed French hornist. The effect of the rancid pie and sauce running down his neck onto his flawless Burberry-clad shoulder was quite awesome, but Tom was not at all perturbed. Muttering apologies, he proceeded to wield his handkerchief vigorously over the mess. Tom's industrious stain-rubbing left any possibility of a successful dry-cleaning effort fairly remote.

The evening was capped off when the bus finally made a bladder relief stop in Marlborough. After a brief interlude, I tracked Tom down in the nearby pub to tell him we were leaving at once, only to find him well into a pint and displaying his famed sculling abilities: opening his throat and pouring it down like a bucket into a gully trap. We had earned quite well from this talent of Tom's. While locals were forced to pay up their losses on bets, their imbursement of Tom's talent was further extended by the fact that they were so lost in admiration that they bought rounds of drink for us over and over again.

You will no doubt have guessed that we missed the bus and were stranded on a particularly frosty night on the cold and lonely streets of Marlborough. We managed to hitch a lift with a rather large truck driver some two hours later and were deposited on the outskirts of London within a couple of miles of a tube. When we finally reached the station, we discovered that we had drunk most of Tom's pub earnings, and the remainder fell short of the required train fares.

Jon Weaving in his Sadler's Wells days

In everyone's opinion, the cleanest and best presented theatre was Her Majesty's in Aberdeen, but a week in Dundee at the Gaumont cinema was a nightmare. My chorus days were over by then, thank the good Lord, as the men had to dress in an attic up many flights of stairs, and were given two buckets of cold water with which to wash off their makeup.

I had proved myself as a tenor of sorts and was feeling much happier about my voice and vocal stamina. The end had come about in Hull when I had been asked to meet Norman Tucker in the company office on a Saturday morning. A few of us had been playing pool and I left in the middle of a (losing) game to go and see what was doing.

He wasted no time in getting to the point. I always felt that he was a rather shy man and he said quite diffidently, that he would like to offer me a principal contract. All my years of dreaming suddenly became reality. I thanked him and left, blushing with embarrassment. I didn't say a word about money.

I went back to the game and told my friends and colleagues what had happened. Then the storm broke! Rather than receiving any form of congratulations, I was abused as being a terrible singer, completely unworthy of the promotion, the worst voice they had ever heard, and so on. The leader of the onslaught was John Darnley, Rita Hunter's husband, who was my special friend and colleague *and* my golfing partner!

Of course I understood their reactions, as ninety per cent of the chorus members, male and female, had the burning ambition to be a principal. Many of the male singers had the absolute conviction that they could sing better than anyone who was singing a leading role. I have never encountered such blatant and aggressive jealousy, before or since. From being friends with just about everyone in the chorus, I went to having just three or four mates.

Chapter Six

*This is a fault common to all singers, that among their friends
they will never sing when they are asked;
unasked, they will never desist.*

Horace

London touring and Sadler's Wells

It was my luck to go on tour immediately with the Sadler's Wells chorus. This was my introduction to the hilarity and horror of 'theatrical digs'.

In the 1950s in Britain and Europe, motels were unheard of. Hotels were booked out from Monday to Friday, months ahead, by commercial travellers. Consequently the only affordable accommodation was on a Sunday night when the company train arrived in the town.

We had been told all of this before arriving in Bradford for the start of the company tour, and had been given the address of a 'nice' theatrical landlady who had accepted our booking for the week. Traversing the back streets of Bradford, we finally found our goal. This was a small single-fronted terrace house of the type known as two-up- and-two-down: two rooms on each floor, the kitchen built as a lean-to at the back, and the toilet at the end of the tiny yard.

The landlady and her husband, who had two children still at home, had accepted myself and the soprano as a married couple, and had also managed to offer accommodation to three members of the orchestra. If this wasn't surprising enough, one of the company's leading tenors arrived five minutes after we did, and was duly shown his domain which consisted of a mattress in a cupboard under the stairs. He had stayed with this family before, three times in fact and was quite happy to sleep under the stairs so he could send more money home to his wife.

Heating? No-one had ever heard of it – and it was the middle of winter! We had been offered full board, which apparently was normal, and we were paying one pound and ten shillings for the privilege. We went downstairs, still in our overcoats, to look for the dining room and the promised Sunday roast dinner.

There were ten of us at the table by the kitchen, each with an empty plate in front of him or her. My memory of the week and the start of my tenor career was the lady of the house bringing out two bowls of steaming boiled potatoes. Then came a bowl with a whole cabbage in it, showing no signs of having been cooked at all. This was followed by watching her struggle through the door with a huge baking dish full of hot oil, which looked as if she had just drained the sump of a car. Placing the dish of fat in front of herself, she proceeded to scoop backwards and forwards with a large spoon, pulling out pieces of tortured gristle and lumps of fat that she duly shared out. Still fishing around in the black depths, she got to my empty plate. Spooning out a particularly nasty looking lump of God-knows-what, she joyfully exclaimed, 'Oh, here's a nice bit', and dropped it like a golf ball onto my plate. Her words still ring in my ears!

Little did I know that, over the years, things would get worse once the relative comforts of London were left behind. There were several standout events in my touring history. One was the company's soprano appealing to me for help when she discovered that the bedroom she had been given in a guest house in Hull had a large hole in the wall behind the head of her bed, which only stopped her viewing the street by virtue of someone having taped a poster over it. It was the sucking in and out of the poster as the wind blew that made her aware of the problem.

Touring was the result of the Arts Council insisting that both Covent Garden and Sadler's Wells opera companies didn't spend all their subsidies in the metropolitan area, and took opera, kicking and screaming, into the provinces every year. Provincial audiences were very appreciative. We seemed to sell out every performance at major centres, such as Manchester, Leeds, Glasgow, Edinburgh, Bristol and Birmingham. These places provided great venues and theatres with proper facilities.

I cannot remember where or when I first met Richard Bonynge. My first meeting with Joan Sutherland was at a dinner arranged for us to be introduced to London's musical fraternity, but Richard was not with her on that occasion. Richard Bonynge and his wife Dame Joan Sutherland are the most highly decorated couple in the world of opera and classical music.

I do remember seeing *Tales of Hoffman* with Richard in Waterford. The very young John Copley was either the director or his assistant and this was our first meeting with him and his remarkable love of opera. Even at that stage, he knew every word of everyone's role and this stood him in good stead.

On one occasion, James Johnston suddenly missed a performance. Jimmy was a leading tenor at Covent Garden, singing major roles, and also had the reputation of being quite a character. Brychan Powell, a young Welsh tenor at the start of a promising career, had been given the role of understudy to Hoffman. Trusting Jimmy's reliability, or through sheer carelessness, Brychan had not learnt the role off by heart. Suddenly he was called upon to perform and of course was not able to go on. The only solution was for him to sing from a music stand in the wings and John Copley played and mimed Hoffman. The other singers found this a memorable and very funny experience as John pranced, preened and acted his heart out.

Everyone who knew John Copley learnt to just sit back and enjoy the endless stream of stories, gossip and general chit-chat that he delivered. We all recognized that there were few opportunities of getting a word in. If I had to choose people for company on a desert island, John would be very high on the list. He is endlessly entertaining and genuinely amusing.

Sadler's Wells decided to be the first company in the world to perform Gilbert and Sullivan when it came out of copyright, and was free of all the stuffy traditions and old-fashioned routines of the past. The D'Oyle Carte Company was in a rut and there was no doubt that change was necessary. I played golf with some of the principal singers and Suzanne Steele and I were friends of John Reid. We heard a lot about what it was like to be hidebound on stage.

Norman Tucker and his assistants decided to give *Iolanthe* a dust-off and the new production was scheduled to commence at the Theatre Royal, Stratford-on-Avon, at one minute past midnight, to celebrate the freedom from the long period of copyright restrictions.

I cannot believe now that I had the gall to go to Peter Hemmings in his office and ask him if he could guarantee that I would not be cast in it. Tolloller is not a great role, but I was just starting out as a tenor and the performance, being a world first, would receive a lot of publicity. However, Peter agreed.

The production was a great success. It was not wildly modern and updated, quite the opposite and it seemed to me that it was just a sparkling new set of costumes and scenery, but with real opera singers. There was some luxury casting and everyone agreed that the orchestra sounded marvellous.

We went to Stratford-on-Avon every year as part of the touring policy and always over the Christmas period. What a cold place! I have never felt so icily chilled and wasn't the only creature to feel the same. I remember watching from my dressing room window the Royal Swan rescuers chopping swans out of the frozen Avon.

Up the road was a pub with a double-sided sign hanging out front. On one side was the name 'The Black Swan' and on the other, 'The Dirty Duck'. We spent many hours there, having a pint and rubbing elbows with Dorothy Tutin and Dame Peggy Ashcroft. The place was packed with famous actors mingling with singers, stage staff, orchestra members and, occasionally, a member of the public.

The conversation was intoxicating and I was always content to just listen and drink in everything including the wonderful English beer that I had by now grown to appreciate. I behaved so badly in early 1954 when trying my first English draft bitter with June Bronhill and her husband at their local, The Red Lion on Barnes Common, that I shrivel up even now at the memory. Like a stupid, brash youth, wet behind the ears, I gave out the usual guff of visiting colonials about the beer being warm, flat and tasteless, and in retrospect I thank the The Red Lion's locals for not treating me with real violence. I came to appreciate the sheer variety of English beers and ales. Thanks to touring, I grew to know and love draft Bass in Yorkshire, Strongarm in Middleburgh, heavy beer in Scotland, Tetley Country to say nothing of the completely individual brews found in country pubs. Maybe in heaven I will stumble across a pub in the middle of nowhere and see two foaming tankards drawn straight from the barrel, carried up the stairs through a cellar trapdoor behind the bar by the landlord of the pub. This would be heaven!

This makes me remember one of the truly strange things that have happened to me in my life. After arriving in London and being at a loss as to how to spend weekends, when sadly one had nothing to spend, we came across a little book at a tube station. Published by Greenline Buses, its title was *Short Walks from Great Missenden* and, over the following weeks, it introduced us to the glorious countryside of Buckinghamshire, the watercress farms of the river Chess, the stiles out of ploughed fields and the beech woods on the ridges.

We selected our first short walk, listed at around five miles, from the book. After what seemed like twenty miles, laboriously following our little map and a pathway through a hedgerow, we literally stumbled across an American couple prostrate in the grass. They looked more exhausted than we did; the dead giveaway was their copy of *Short Walks* lying in the grass beside them. They gave us the bad news that the five-mile walk was outwards, and then there were another five to negotiate to get back to Great Missenden Station. We were young and foolish, as the song goes, and pressed on. Our turning point was to be a watercress farm where afternoon tea was offered. It was idyllically situated on the Little River Chess and we enthusiastically recorded the event with our camera.

On the walk back, the light was beginning to fade and a bluish mist was settling on the bluebells. We were walking along a ridge through a beech wood when we suddenly came across an old black beam and white plaster pub. The thing that struck us at once was that it had a bent chimney, rather like an oast house and there was smoke wafting from the chimney, mixing with the mist. It looked somehow as if the scene belonged in a fairy tale. The whole impression was of a building gently sinking into the grass. The corners had sunk, and the front door was crooked. Faded gold letters on the black sign told us that it was 'The Leather Bottle'. We were tired and thirsty and it looked very inviting, but we had to get back to the train before dark so we pressed on. We decided that we would have to come back another time and visit.

Two or three weeks later, the walk we had chosen took us very near to our first stroll. We realized that a short detour would take us up into the woods to 'The Leather Bottle', and we could get a snack and a drink. We retraced the path that we had struggled along just a short couple of weeks earlier. As we approached the exact spot, we saw there was no pub. We went into the trees, thinking that it must have burnt down or it had collapsed and we would find the foundations, but there was absolutely nothing to be found. Genuinely shocked, we walked down through a ploughed field to the road where we had seen a small garage and petrol pump. The owner had lived in the area for some time. Neither the man nor his son had ever heard of a pub called 'The Leather Bottle'. This gave us food for thought and, over the next weeks and many journeys around the general area, we never missed an opportunity of asking about the mysterious disappearing hotel. Locals could reel off the names of dozens of pubs in the area but only one old man thought that he could vaguely remember his father mentioning 'The Leather Bottle' at some time in the distant past. I wonder what would have happened if we had gone in.

Chapter Seven

*It is the best of all trades, to make songs,
and the second best to sing them.*
Hilaire Belloc

The beginnings of success

Success was beginning to come my way, but the plans of the Sadler's Wells management were not working out quite so well. The goal was a permanent move to the Coliseum Theatre in St Martin's Lane. The Company mounted an absolutely splendid production of Lehár's *Land of Smiles*. Sou Chong, the leading tenor role, had been written for Richard Tauber and he had introduced it to London with great success. The title refers to the Chinese custom of smiling whatever happens in life.

Our production was to star the English tenor Charles Craig who, after years as the stalwart of the Carl Rosa Opera, was finally being recognized as more than worthy of a permanent place on London stages. After years of constant touring this was a much appreciated change.

The role of the Chinese prince Sou Chong is known in the trade as the operetta tenor's Tristan, as it is by operetta standards a very long and demanding role. As the production was scheduled to play eight times a week, it was necessary to cast another tenor in the same role to allow the two to alternate.

The lovely Australian soprano Elizabeth Fretwell was to sing Lisa and by coincidence, Sou Chong number two was another Australian, Ronald Dowd, a fine intelligent singer. Ron was nevertheless known amongst his colleagues as 'Rowdy Dowdy'. I understood why after meeting him for the first time in 'The Shakespeare', the Wells stage-door pub. Our group had been talking cricket and my first remark to Ron was, 'What fantastic weather we are having', referring to the games we had played recently. His forefinger in my chest drove me back against the wall, his face inches from mine.

'I don't think it's good weather. I think it is bloody awful weather!' and so on.

This was the reaction I would have expected had I mortally insulted his mother, but I learned over time that this was fairly normal for Rowdy. A small group of Australians played squash every week and to get on the court against Ron or John Shaw was very dangerous. There was no quarter given by either gentleman. When making a backswing, it was not unusual for either of them to raise a weal across the bridge of their opponent's nose. On the other hand, Ron gave me some valuable advice about forging my burgeoning career. Some of the advice, however, involved being told to hammer on desks and demand roles. Forty years later I have still not managed to get around to trying that charming tactic.

I was still officially a chorus member but was chosen with South African Lawrence Folley, a great friend and colleague, to sing a trio in the first act with Covent Garden's Barbara Howitt. I don't know how they found this piece for Barbara, as I have sung dozens of performances as Sou Chong in several different productions over the years since, and have never known of this trio in any other production.

Lawrie and I were to be Hussars in the opening scene of Act One, set in aristocratic Vienna. I can honestly say neither of us had ever looked better on stage. The costumes were in black and white with shiny black boots and tailored to form-fitting perfection. Both of us were well over six feet tall and very slim. Having one of us on each side of Barbara helped to persuade the audience that we were much stronger trio than we actually were.

Land of Smiles has never been a hit with the public, compared with huge Lehár successes like *The Merry Widow* and *The Count of Luxembourg*. Perhaps it is true that the sad ending is not the expected climax of a night at the operetta in which normally – quite unlike grand opera – nobody dies. Unfortunately the show's record proved this to be true and the box-office returns were not good enough after the first two weeks.

One of the star principal singers when I first started going to Sadler's Wells' performances was Denis Dowling. Apart from a fine baritone, he had a wonderfully nasally resonant, speaking voice. I had had no acting or movement lessons, although I did learn to faint on stage at the opera school that I attended for a short few weeks as a youth in Melbourne. Because of my lack of formal training I was greatly impressed by Denis Dowling and chose him as my model for the future. He had elegance and a way of moving and behaving on stage that I was determined to copy.

Whenever I had the chance I would watch what he did and try to work out how he did it so well. Later, when actually appearing with him, I found myself acutely aware of what he was doing and continued to learn from his stagecraft. He also did some terrible things. I well remember in *Merrie England* when he got lost in the famous Friar Tuck patter solo about the sturgeon and stickleback, so lost that he endlessly repeated the same words. Someone behind me on stage muttered quite audibly that it would have been kinder to shoot him. Whether Denis took this amiss, believing it had been me making that remark, I don't know. In the finale at the end of my fight with quarterstaves against Long John, the action required me to be sent sprawling across the stage into Friar Tuck's ample gut, and the two of us would fall in a heap. While I was getting to my feet, Denis quietly removed my wig. All I could do was shove him into the wings, retrieve the ornate Walter Raleigh headpiece, drape it on any old how and get back on stage.

Losing a wig on stage is not such a rare occurrence and a beard falling off is also a well-known sight. I have always had an absolute loathing of spirit gum, the standard theatrical adhesive for hairpieces. Whenever possible and given the time, I have grown a beard to avoid the sickening discomfort of having glue painted on my skin. For roles such as Pluto in *Orpheus in the Underworld* and Gardefeu in *La Vie Parisienne*, I was thus able to approach my makeup table with equanimity. Naturally, growing a beard was not always possible and I used to experiment with all sorts of adhesives.

Once, in Stratford-on-Avon at the Royal Shakespeare Theatre, I thought I had hit the jackpot with the discovery of a tube of French latex adhesive. This was not unpleasant to use and I attached Pluto's blue and white feathered beard easily. It remained charmingly in place until the middle of my entrance song when the lights started to play a part and, combined with my perspiration, managed to begin turning the latex glue into oil. I could feel the beard slipping, first one side and then the other, and I must have looked remarkably sage finishing the scene holding my chin with thumb and forefinger of one hand while the other hand held my large golden hat on to a rapidly loosening feather wig.

When a singer wears a moustache on stage it is usually in two halves to allow the top lip freedom and flexibility. Dino Borgioli told me once that soprano Toti Dal Monte had a favourite trick of standing in the crook of a tenor's arm, looking up at him and whispering that his moustache had come off. Looking down his nose the tenor usually saw one end, and assuming that the other had gone, pulled it off quickly. I know tenors are thick but I could never understand why they couldn't see both ends and why this gag worked. But Dino said many tenors went off stage to find themselves wearing half a moustache. There are well-known stories of tenors swallowing their moustache. Walter Midgely at Covent Garden was one.

The best hairy upper lip story I know is what happened when Gloria Lane came from New York to sing *Carmen* at the Wells during a touring opera season.

Gloria created a sensation during her first performance when she did a 'Sharon Stone'. Sitting with her legs apart and her hands tied behind her back, preparing to start the seguidilla, she leaned forward, took her skirt in her teeth and sat back against the wall. This may have been the one time that Don Jose was genuinely persuaded to release her. Gloria did another few things that first night, including describing in a stream of lurid four-letter words the conductor's ability during the introduction to the habanera.

But back to moustaches. The male chorus had to kneel in a half-circle around the seated Carmen, backs to the audience, after the applause for the habanera died down. At this point they were to sing 'Carmen, every man you see here is your slave'.

Instead they temporarily removed half of their moustaches and, with their backs to the audience, sang 'Carmen, every man you see here needs a shave', sending Gloria into convulsions.

There is a story that the Canadian baritone Louis Quilico, while singing an aria in Buenos Aires, threw back his head to sing the last note, took a deep breath and swallowed not his moustache but the white feather which some of the audience had noted wafting teasingly down from the flies. He fainted in the middle of the stage in front of the prompt box and the curtain was hastily closed. The highly excitable Latin stage manager rushed from his corner to make an apology to the audience. In stepping through the curtain he tripped over Louis's inert form, fell into the orchestra pit and broke his leg.

The opening night of the Sadler's Wells production of *Orpheus in the Underworld* was one of the most exciting nights of the 1960 London opera season. This was the unanimous opinion of the London and world theatre critics.

The 'Wells' had long wanted a larger theatre and had made an experimental foray into the heart of London's West End with a short season of classical operetta at the magnificent Coliseum. There were wonderful productions of *Die Fledermaus* and Lehár's *Land of Smiles*, the latter not having been seen in the UK since Richard Tauber's portrayal of Prince Sou Chong. As I mentioned previously, the role of Prince Sou Chong is known in the trade as the operetta tenor's Tristan. As I later discovered in various productions on the continent, it is a good description. When I was performing the role on alternate nights with Rudolph Schock, he told me he would 'rather be singing *Lohengrin* for a rest'.

After this production folded, *The Merry Widow* was revived and this was the first of the many hundred times I played Danilo. In this production, the widow was played by June Bronhill. This was a huge success with the public but the short lease of the theatre was up and the company returned to its famous Roseberry Avenue home.

Chapter Eight

Singing is the ultimate do-it-yourself activity. No one can do it for you.

Orpheus in the Underworld

It was at this time I met a vivacious lady named Wendy Toye CBE. Wendy was a British dancer, and stage and film director. She told me that she had something wonderful planned for me in what was, for the moment, a secret new production. I was reminded of this meeting when some time later (and well into the various runs of life on Olympus, and somewhat lower in Pluto's Underworld), she came into my dressing room, laughing out loud. It was her practice to pop into the Wells every now and then during performance and stand at the back of the dress circle to check that the standard was being kept up, also – it appeared to me – to check on my body make-up. She often complained that I had been lazy with applying enough to my legs and back. Pluto's make-up was a nightmare as the costume was very skimpy and a fair proportion of my costume was Max Factor, blue and red sequins, and coloured feathers. I was always the last out of the stage door and into the Shakespeare pub, but the same small group would be waiting. They were proud of never missing a performance.

The cause of Wendy's mirth was that as soon as the overture commenced, one of the old ladies sitting in front of her turned to her companion and in a shocked, very audible whisper announced: 'But this isn't Gluck's *Orpheus*!'

Well, wasn't that just the truth. Offenbach had created another of his glorious send-ups of Greek mythology and the team of Wendy Toye, Geoffrey Dunn as librettist and Malcolm Pride's superbly beautiful and imaginative scenery and costumes had done Cologne's favourite son proud. The public could not get enough of this production and, rather than be part of the opera season, it was finally performed 'en suite' with seven performances a week.

Like a West End musical, *Orpheus* had out of town try-outs and the first nearly caused a genuine inferno. Pluto disguised as the local deity Aristaeus (in charge of oil and honey), entices Eurydice into a cornfield by changing costume and becoming an even more attractive figure. Under a huge shepherd's smock and an enormous hat lurked the nearly naked Pluto in his purple feathered head-dress. I had to invite Eurydice to 'look at me now' and duck down behind the sheaves of corn and change in an enormous puff of smoke and light. This worked without a hitch. Suitably impressed, June Bronhill agreed to go down below with me and we exited. Suddenly mixed laughter and sounds of alarm started in the auditorium as the cornfield caught fire. I had dropped my hat on top of one of the smoke boxes and the charge had exploded it into life. It must have been very funny to see Orpheus run on stage and pick up the hat on the end of his violin bow and exit into the wings like a flaming meteor, whilst a fireman entered and sprayed the corn. Now that would have been good publicity for a new production about the underworld!

It seemed in the 1950s and 1960s that the roster of principal singers at Covent Garden and the Wells was largely made up of Australians, New Zealanders and Canadians. I had a theory about this and believed that singers from overseas just had to succeed. They were not living comfortably in the family nest – far from it – and, as students in London, endured pretty rough living quarters and financial stress. There was a real sink or swim attitude shown by the immigrants and a fair bit of resentment shown by the local singers. I remember a performance of *Die Fledermaus* when Frederick Sharpe as the Governor Frank was confronted by Adele (June Bronhill). She told him that she 'wanted to be an actress'. His line should have been 'But have you any talent?' Jimmy added, 'or did you come over by ship?'

Before the transformation, Jon in *Orpheus in the Underworld*, London, 1960

Jon as Pluto, *Orpheus in the Underworld*, London, 1960

No-one should be surprised then to hear that the main roles in *Orpheus* were mostly cast with Australians. June was Eurydice, Kevin Miller as Orpheus, myself as Pluto, Margaret Nisbett as Cupid and we were coupled with Alan Crowfoot, a Canadian, as Styx and Suzanne Steele from South Africa as Diana.

The Garnet Carroll organization invited some of the principals to tour Australia in *Orpheus* and *The Merry Widow*. An Australian orchestra, chorus, and minor principals supported six or seven of the London cast, and toured as the Sadler's Wells Company. This proved to be a huge commercial success and the thirteen-week contract ran into three years! The success of the season may be judged by the final night in Sydney. The famous can-can in the *Orpheus* finale was always encored; on the final night, thirteen times. I used to advance to the footlights and crack my whip at the audience in pretended impatience at wanting to get on with the show and my shoulder was starting to ache. Goodness knows how the dancers, let alone the orchestra and singers, survived that night.

An ironical sidelight: in 1969 I was singing Bacchus in *Ariadne auf Naxos* at the Coliseum, the new home of the English National Opera into which Sadler's Wells had morphed and the musical director Charles Mackerras had the idea that I should recreate Pluto on my 'free' nights. It was a chance to reunite with the wonderful Eric Shilling. Eric was an English opera singer and producer noted for his impeccable diction and mastery of stagecraft. But the season was a sad one for me. There were just too many memories of the original cast. Too many great characters were missing and too many wonderful details ignored. It was certainly an enormous contrast to sing so many *Rings* on the same stage after performing in so many *Widows* and *Orpheuses*. I sang *Las Vie Parisienne, Raoul de Gardefeu, La Belle Helene* and *Hoffman* but the Offenbach closest to my heart is *Orpheus*. I wish the company 'Toi Toi Toi!' with this treasure.

Jon as Hoffman in *Hoffman's Erzählungen*, Kiel, 1969

Chapter Nine

No matter how naturally talented and individual singer may be, he or she cannot produce the best result without a proper and sufficiently long course of training.

Enrico Caruso

Touring Australia, 1962–66

It was a shock when I read the small print on my contract and discovered that I was in Australia for the 'run of the shows', *Orpheus in the Underworld* and *The Merry Widow*.

Eric Shilling and Kevin Miller left for London after thirteen weeks and I missed them both on stage and off. As I write this [2006], I have just heard that Eric has died. He was a great colleague, which is terribly important on long runs, and nobody would dispute his talent as a character singer. My first experience of his singing was as Daland in Wagner's *Flying Dutchman* but that was perhaps not really his thing. We first sang together in *Die Fledermaus*, when he was a most excellent Frank, the prison Governor. To me, his starring role was as Jupiter in Offenbach's *Orpheus*. Who could forget his blue feathered beard bristling upwards as he fought with Juno before finally resigning himself to his wife's wishes? As to his transformation into a blowfly and his 'buzz, buzz, buzz' duet with Euridice in Act Three, one can only say 'unforgettable'.

I bought the latest eight-millimetre movie camera and took it next door into Eric and Kevin's shared dressing room at the Wells. They both immediately asked me to buy them one. We were just born too early; we now have reels and reels of performances and backstage goings-on but with no sound. If only we had been able to use a modern video camera, what memories we would have preserved.

Orpheus in the Underworld opened at the Tivoli in Sydney in August 1962 and a wonderful new chapter opened in my life. Before leaving for London in the early 1950s, I had only once been outside Victoria. Arriving in Sydney was for me like being allowed into a land of lotus eaters. I have the same feeling in California, but without the calm of being at home. To this day I find the whole atmosphere of Sydney electric. Is it the sea air, the constant harbour views, the different light, the glorious Pacific coastline? In 1962, all this was coupled with starring in a hit show, which in itself is a rousing thing. Capping it all was the discovery of Sydney's North Shore.

I was invited to a private club for lunch at Palm Beach on my first Sunday, the first of many precious free days. The drive up the coast from Manly took a magical turn as I suddenly saw what appeared to be a little palm oasis down on the beach, and the die was cast. It was my first sight of Bilgola. The day at Palm Beach was fine but my mind was set on the spot I had seen just a few kilometres back, and I knew I had to live there. Not so easy though, as there were only a few houses down on the sand. I was not too unhappy to be able to lease a house up on the cliff on the Serpentine. The views were magnificent looking south down the coast. The roar and thump of the surf was so enjoyable that I didn't want to miss the sound by sleeping at night and I spent hours out on the deck under the stars.

Australian tour of Sadler's Wells' production of *Orpheus in the Underworld*, Sydney, 1962

Chapter Ten

*To my beloved Monique.
Without her urging, these memories would have
remained in my head.*

Preparing for a European career

There are two ways of being contracted to an opera company. One is to be 'fest engagiert'. This means you are engaged for fifty-two weeks in the year. The other, when one is more successful, is to be engaged as a guest for a certain role. The latter has become more common as opera houses try to economise and endeavor to divest themselves of certain responsibilities such as holidays and sick pay. As a guest, you sing or you don't earn.

These days the position is almost reversed and a young singer does not have the luxury of yearly security. The two choices appear to be an apprenticeship in a 'young artists' programme, or being engaged on a guest contract for a certain number of weeks' rehearsal and a set number of performances.

A permanent house contract for one or two years allows a singer the luxuries of a regular income, paid holidays, sick pay, pension scheme etc. It is like working in a bank, although I imagine just a little bit more exciting. A permanent contract can allow a singer to have days, sometimes even weeks, free from performances and still receive a monthly cheque. When the European winter takes its toll and colds and flu are rife, one can be off sick without any worries... except whether your understudy is dangerously good!

I knew nothing about the European system of getting an engagement. In 1966 in Australia we only knew that we wanted to break into Germany, Austria or Switzerland but had no idea how to go about it. Suzanne and I were in Sydney and I phoned a friend, Robert Allman, the great baritone, who I have always considered to be Australia's answer to Leonard Warren, who was acknowledged by critics to be among the world's best dramatic baritones. Rob and I go way back: in Melbourne at opera school in the early 1950s we appeared together in *Cosi Fan Tutte* with me singing the bass role of Don Alfonso to his Gugliemo.

Our roles were soon to be reversed, he to be the baritone and me the tenor. He went on to have a marvellous career at Covent Garden Royal Opera and leading opera houses on the continent before returning home to be one of the linch pins of the young Australian company. He sang eleven roles alongside Joan Sutherland and was principal artist with Opera Australia. He was appointed an Officer of the Order of the British Empire and a member of the order of Australia.

When you want information, take your source to dinner. Bob was very generous with his knowledge, and really put us in the picture about the whole rigmarole of getting an agent, an audition and hopefully an engagement. His advice was invaluable.

The system worked like this. First you had to sing for an agent, and most of them were in Munich and Vienna. Bob Allmann recommended two in Munich as being the best. It appeared that Robert Schulz and Harry Schmidt had been partners, broken up and now had their suites of offices just around the corner from each other. We were advised to be discreet and only approach one of the gentlemen.

One meets so many different types of people in the theatrical world. Some are in the profession for all the wrong reasons, notably money and fame. The administrators are often just plain empire-building and seeking power. But generally, most are doing what they do for artistic reasons.

Among singers, conductors and directors (and by directors I mean *regisseurs*) there are some really bad apples, and you hope that you never have to work with them again, although they do keep turning up in the strangest places. One man, who was an absolute monster, turned out to be engaged with me for a season in Namibia, of all places, and there was no escaping him. I just prayed that a lion would eat him and be able to digest the meal. I couldn't.

Rita Hunter was one of the majority. She was a lovely colleague who got on with whatever was happening and didn't make a fuss. Friendly to everyone, funny at rehearsals with her sly humour, and a marvellous performer who seemingly never had an off night, Rita was sadly missed when she finally retired.

I first became aware of Rita in about 1956 during a performance of *The Barber of Seville*, performed by the Carl Rosa Opera in Peterborough. Richard Bonynge and I caught a milk train from London to be there in time for the performance. If I may diverge a little from Rita and talk about the Carl Rosa Company, the performance and its highlights made the interminable milk train journey worth every hour of it. Almaviva sang his serenade to Rosina and she was duly dragged away from the window by Bartolo. So far so good. But surprisingly, the Dr Bartolo was Harry Powell Lloyd, the director, and known to us all as the husband of Covent Garden's great mezzo, Edith Coates. The surprise was compounded by the fact that Dr Bartolo was wearing a Harris tweed sports jacket and even those attending their first operatic performance must have noticed that his wig was on backwards. He glared out of the window and then retreated to allow the performance to continue as Rossini intended. Intrigued by this turn of events, Rick and I went backstage at interval to ask what was going on. The programme had informed us that Joseph Sartariano, one of the Carl Rosa's stalwarts and a truly great Rigoletto, was supposed to be the afternoon's Bartolo. He was famous for spending his spare time when on tour with the Carl Rosa Company in buying up pianos and shipping them off to his brother in Malta.

After discovering his absence from the stage a search party was sent out. They discovered him pushing a piano on a small trolley down the main street of Peterborough on his way to the station. His reply to their consternation was, 'Whatsa da problem...I only missed the first act.'

The sequel to this story is that some years later his brother cabled him and it read something like, 'Stop sending pianos! We now have more pianos than people on Gozo.'

The Almaviva in this performance was the Adelaide tenor, Kevin Miller. Margaret Nisbett was the Rosina and the Figaro was John Heddle Nash, son of the great tenor who spent the war years in Australia, so we were very well represented.

The revelation of the third act was a Miss Rita Hunter as Bertha, whose aria performance was a knockout. As she was sharing a dressing room with Margaret, we were able to congratulate her heartily and have a nice chat. From then on I was able to follow Rita's career closely and although in the same company – later Sadler's Wells Opera – the fact that we were never cast in the same opera allowed me to watch and listen from out front. As we all know, she sang a large number of leading roles, but the one that sticks in my memory from that period was her portrayal of the Owl in *Cunning Little Vixen*. Who could ever forget Rita as this enormous brown owl perched on a log and flapping her wings. At the first stage costume rehearsal everyone, including Rita, was hysterical with laughter.

It is fairly well documented that Sadler's Wells let three sopranos go because of their size. Two were Jane and Milly from the chorus, and they were crying for days. I didn't see Rita for a time and, because

Jon's Solo

I came home to Melbourne with the Sadler's Wells tour in 1962, we lost touch. Back in London in the late 1960s I was driving along St Martin's Lane, passing the Coliseum, and there was Rita coming out of the front door. I discovered that she was back in favour and back in the fold. It is opera history now that she was one of the pillars on which the English National Opera's *Ring* was built, and this is how we finally came to sing together.

Charles Mackerras had engaged me for the 1969 season to sing *Force of Destiny* and the Irish tenor Hugh Beresford, who was singing *Tannhäuser* at Bayreuth, was to sing Bacchus in *Ariadne auf Naxos*.

Three weeks before the premieres, Charles Mackerras rang me in Germany and told me that Hugh couldn't manage the role. He asked if I would agree to swap premieres with Hugh. I most unwisely agreed to do so and fell victim to the fact that anyone worth their salt can learn a role musically in hours but it takes months to get it into the voice and the voice muscles. I went to Salzburg to enlist the coaching talents of Max Lorenz and his first question was, how long did we have to prepare? He was most concerned when I told him it was two and a half weeks. We got on with it and he was marvellous. When, at the conclusion of our time together, I wanted to pay him, he said, 'I believe so much in your future success that I would not think of accepting anything financial. Just keep in touch and let me know how everything is going.'

There is an interesting story about *Forces of Destiny*, the opera written by Guiseppe Verdi in 1861. The American baritone Leonard Warren had a cerebral haemorrhage and died during Act Three. The aria he was about to sing begins with 'Morir, tremenda cosa' ('to die, a momentous thing'). He was only forty-eight years old. Pavarotti and many old-school Italian singers avoided playing Alvaro, believing the role was cursed and to sing it brought bad luck.

In Paris I had asked Domenic Modesti's wife, who was a flower maiden at Bayreuth, what it was like to hear Franz Volker, the German dramatic tenor who excelled specifically as a performer of

Music and Love

the operas of Richard Wagner. I had been told his voice expressed warmth, strength and sensitivity. She told me it was as if he was bouncing his voice off the back walls of the theatre like a tennis ball. Max told me that one of Volker's rivals and colleagues had described him as follows: 'Sah aus wie ein frankfurter Schlachter, und war so schtink langweilig.' ('He looked like a Frankfurt slaughterman, and was bloody boring.')

There are many people I am grateful to and one of these was my cousin Ken Neate. He was the tenor at Joan Sutherland's first Covent Garden performance of *Lucia di Lammermoor* and also sang Loge at Bayreuth and Tristan with Birgit Nilsson in Vienna.

Ken Neate, Jon's cousin

Ken was the man who told Lord Harewood that if I were to take up his offer to sing both Siegfrieds, I would need one and a half years to study the role. As I was so busy with other performances on the continent, he should consider sending a repetiteur to live with me and work on the roles whenever I was free. I am eternally grateful to Charles Mackerras and George Harewood that they agreed. They sent Len Hancock, an old friend from Sadler's Wells days, who conducted the first performance of Vaughan William's *Pilgrim's Progress* at Covent Garden, to live with me. My performances were a success but they were not so for the Brünnhilde, and she never sang the role again for the English National Opera.

Charles Mackerras CBE was an Australian conductor and an authority on operas of Janacek and Mozart. He became principal conductor of the BBC Concert Orchestra. George Henry Hubert

Lascelles, 7th Earl of Harewood, has had an interesting life. Sixth in line to the British throne, he was a music enthusiast and devoted most of his career to opera. He was director of the Royal Opera House, Covent Garden. He fought in Algeria and Italy during World War II, and in 1944 was captured by the Germans and kept prisoner at Colditz until 1945. Adolf Hitler signed his death warrant. The SS general commanding the camp, realizing the war was lost, refused to carry out the sentence and released him to the Swiss. In 1956 he took his seat in the House of Lords and Queen Elizabeth II created him a Knight Commander of the Order of the British Empire.

Richard Wagner's *Der Ring des Nibelungen* is a cycle of four epic operas: in sequence, *Das Rheingold*, *Die Walküre*, *Siegfried* and *Götterdämmerung*. A full performance of the *Ring*, about fifteen hours in total, takes place over four nights at the opera. Occasionally one of the four is performed separately, although the composer intended them to be performed as a series. The story is modelled after ancient Greek dramas, and the scale and scope of the story is epic. It follows the struggles of gods, heroes, and several mythical creatures over the eponymous magic *Ring* that grants domination over the entire world.

The music of the cycle is thick and richly textured, and becomes more complex as the cycle proceeds. Wagner wrote for an orchestra of gargantuan proportions, including a greatly enlarged brass section. He eventually had a purpose-built theatre constructed, the Bayreuth Festspielhaus, in which to perform this work. The theatre has a special stage that blends the huge orchestra with the singers' voices, allowing them to sing at a natural volume. The result was that the singers did not have to strain themselves vocally during the long performances.

I sang the *Ring* cycle for several years with Rita. Alberto Remedios and I alternated in the cycles. If I sang Siegmund in one, he sang the Siegfrieds. Then we changed and I had Rita as my lady love and Alberto was my Father in the second cycle. Poor Rita. She never sang the Immolation to the correct Siegfried. One of the most unpleasant experiences was wearing a death mask and being encased in plaster with a breathing tube to help me survive as I lay 'dead' for quite some time. In so many other productions later on, I was killed, carried off and then brought back to lie at Brünnhilde's feet. There I would remain immobile for the whole of the Immolation, trying not to wince at the splashes of saliva from overhead. This is one of my life's discoveries – all sopranos spit when they sing!

Alberto and I both had our death masks and the English National Opera *Ring* called for a dummy Siegfried to lie on the funeral pyre and have everything collapse on top of him, in the opera's finale. It was someone's job to change the mask to correspond with whoever was playing Siegfried. To my knowledge, no-one ever got it right. After singing my heart out for hours I would stand in the wings and watch Rita pour her heart out over the body with Alberto's face, but this never seemed apparent to the audience. The Coliseum is so enormous that it was completely unnecessary to make two masks.

The two so-called male and female star dressing rooms at the Coliseum had a communicating door. Rita and I liked to have the door open to allow us to chat while making up and dressing, and also later during the long wait through the Norns scene in *Götterdämmerung*. However, in *Siegfried* she came on later in the performance. I would have been working for some hours already, and literally only meet her on stage when I climbed the fiberglass mountain to find her sleeping under her shield. Kneeling down to kiss her after the great deliberation as to whether it was safe to do so, I would always murmur, 'Hi, Reet, how are you?' as I bent to kiss her. It has been said before, but how unfair it is for Siegfried to sing for over an hour and a half, then to awaken the soprano, who is as fresh as a daisy and who proceeds to sing him off the stage. This is the problem that Wagner set his tenors.

Jon as Lohengrin, in *Lohengrin*, Kiel, 1968

Jon as Siegmund in *Die Walküre*, English National Opera, London, 1973–77

Jon as Siegfried in *Siegfried* with Rita Hunter, London, 1974

Incidentally, the first Siegfried I ever sang in German was in Wiesbaden with Leonie Rysanek, the Austrian dramatic soprano. She came into my dressing room and said, 'I have recently had a nasty car accident, so when you kiss me awake, would you help me to my feet?' You can imagine my dismay. It must have seemed a bit ridiculous to see me help Brünnhilde up, face to face, and then run away to hide behind a rock while she asks who has woken her. Leonie's endurance in the high tessitura of Strauss's operas is legendary. She only sang Brünnhilde once; she said her respect for her colleague Birgit Nilsson led to her avoidance of Birgit's signature role.

Rita and I had a good giggle one night when Norman Bailey came down Ralph Koltai's fibreglass mountain like a skier, not moving a muscle, just gliding on feet firmly planted and singing away quite normally. Apart from getting stuck in the tubular globe of the world through which we entered for the *Götterdämmerung* love duet, I can't remember anything very untoward happening to the two of us. I did split my suede trousers from front to back in the first act of *Die Walküre*, when I fell to the floor in front of the hearth, but this situation was repaired before Rita appeared in Act Two to tell me I was going to die. Too late – I had already died from embarrassment in Act One.

I wish I could tell Rita how much we all admired her great talent and how much we still admire it. She was a marvellous colleague and it was a pleasure to know her, and to sing with her. She was awarded the Commander of the British Empire and died in Sydney in 2001, aged 67.

Chapter Eleven

Without music, life would be a mistake.
Friedrich Nietzsche

Coda

Jon died on 19 October 2011.

Due to his illness, Jon's account of his life concludes around 1967. This was two years before Jon and I met while performing *The Merry Widow*.

Jon left Australia and went to Europe where he auditioned in different opera houses in Austria and Germany. He eventually signed a 'fest Vertrag' (a full-time contract) with the Kiel Opera in August 1967.

It was in 1967 that Jon changed from performing as an 'all rounder', singing on television, in musicals, and operettas, to become a 'Heldentenor' – that is, a heroic tenor. These are the voices that are required in order to sing the demanding tenor roles in the works of Wagner and in other German romantic operas.

His first role in Kiel was the title role in Wagner's *Lohengrin*, a part that suited him like a glove! He loved it and so did the audience. It was a huge success. This period was a very happy and rewarding time for Jon. It was a great opera house, he enjoyed lovely colleagues and fantastic roles, and the opera house was in a nice city by the sea.

He sang many great opera roles including Othello in Verdi's *Othello,* Hoffmann in Offenbach's *Hoffmann's Erzählungen,* Faust in Gounod's *Margarethe,* and Florestan in Beethoven's *Fidelio,* among many others. Jon stayed in Kiel until we moved to Augsburg in 1971.

Jon as Bacchus in *Ariadne of Naxos,*
English National Opera, London, 1973

He performed the *Ring* cycle with the English National Opera at the Coliseum in London from 1973 to 1977.

While Jon was writing this account of his life and work, from time to time he would recall an episode, event or particular performance in some detail. A great raconteur, he would entertain our family and guests with these wonderful stories. Fortunately, he wrote some down for inclusion in later chapters of his autobiography – chapters that, sadly, he did not have the time to write. Here is Jon's account of the moment when the idea of living permanently in Australia first struck him.

Jon as Florestan in *Fidelio*, Cape Town, 1981

One of my most unusual engagements began when my London agent phoned me in Melbourne and asked if I was free and interested in going to perform in Namibia. Well, for a start, I was not at all sure where Namibia was! Learning that it was the former German colony in south-west Africa, I immediately became very interested indeed. I had spent many happy weeks singing Florestan in Beethoven's *Fidelio* in South Africa with the Cape Town Opera.

I had just finished singing Siegfried at the Leipzig Opera and began my journey to Namibia by taking the train to East Berlin. Transferring to West Berlin's Templehof airport was the usual maddening adventure thanks to Erich Honecker's border guards, but somehow I managed to make the Pan Am flight to Hamburg. Pan Am seemed to have a monopoly on flights to West Germany. Whether this was true or not, they were certainly pretty complacent about their standard of service. True to form, a stewardess managed to drop a cup of scalding hot coffee in my lap and I spent the last fifteen minutes of the flight quietly seething and steaming.

I was to meet Monique at Hamburg airport and pick up a suitcase of clean clothes, change planes for Frankfurt, and then take the South African Airways flight to Johannesburg. It was not easy for Monique to bring my case to the airport, as she had a performance that night at the Operettenhaus on Hamburg's infamous Reeperbahn. It was to be the final performance given there before the theatre closed for renovations to enable it to accommodate *Phantom of the Opera* with Peter Hoffman.

She was standing in the arrivals hall with a suitcase at her feet and Jack in her arms when I emerged with my luggage. The Pan Am flight had arrived late, and I had to get in line quickly for the Frankfurt flight. There was nothing for it but to change my trousers while standing in the queue in the middle of the departure hall. Despite the interest this caused, I proceeded to do just that. Standing there with my pants around my ankles, I said to Monique, 'We can't live like this!' The first real thought of returning permanently to Australia was born.

How I wish that Jon could have finished his story, and that we might have enjoyed more years of love and music together.

Monique's Solo

Chapter One

I sing therefore I am

The invisible tenor

I'm in London, at the Wigmore Hall studios, on 21 May 1962. I can hear a wonderful tenor voice: 'I'm off to Chez Maxim...'

I'm leaning my back against the wall, embraced by the warmth of the glorious sounds streaming through the wall from the studio next door. With my eyes closed, I begin to picture the person who is producing those wonderful sounds. I feel the voice engulfing my body and reaching my soul. I feel this man in my heart and imagine him to be big, dark and full of strength and warmth.

Every day, for the next three months, while waiting to see my singing coach, Mme Triguez, I listened to that voice. I became obsessed with hearing the marvellous music coming from the invisible tenor and was disappointed if I did not hear him. I listened eagerly to his exciting voice rendering the most interesting songs and arias with amazing ease.

At that time I did not know that the great coach, Audrey Langford, was teaching the invisible tenor in the other studio and she would become my coach eight years later.

Audrey Langford was a very knowledgeable and highly sought-after singing teacher in London and we became close friends in the

1970s. She often mentioned the importance of singers keeping their own teeth. An embarrassing incident happened in one of our lessons that confirmed her comments. During the lesson, Audrey put her hand up to her face, demonstrating how the voice should be rushing free out of one's mouth. Instead of her sound rushing out, her teeth did, and landed on the keyboard. Stunned, I pretended to look out the window but out of the corner of my eye I saw Audrey pick up her teeth, and without comment put them back where they belonged.

Most importantly, I did not know that the invisible tenor was going to be my partner for more than half my life, and the father of my only child.

Who was this man? I had to wait until 2 January 1969, almost seven years later, to get the answer.

I was thrilled to be asked to audition for a production of *The Merry Widow* in Kiel, and delighted to be offered the part. All my hard work was showing a result! Unfortunately, the tenor who was contracted to the Kiel Opera had declined – he had sung Danilo more often than any other tenor in the world, and was no longer wanting to sing operetta. He had recently been singing the lead in Wagner's *Lohengrin*, and I found it hard to imagine a Wagnerian tenor singing Danilo in any case.

Life takes unexpected twists and turns. Weeks after this audition, and still not having heard who would be singing the tenor role, I met a charming gentleman on a train to Munich. A baritone working in Kiel, he was most interested in my story of *The Merry Widow* problem. A twist: the tenor who had refused the role of Danilo was a close friend of his, and he had heard all about it. In what was to be a fateful turn of events, the baritone mentioned to the tenor that he had met the Widow.

Whatever the baritone said to the tenor about the Widow, the tenor changed his mind and accepted the role in the production that was to begin in January 1969. The tenor was, of course, Jon. His teacher at Wigmore Hall was Audrey Langford.

The story of our face-to-face meeting in Kiel is told later in this book. In between I had so many engagements to sing, so many roles to learn, so many lessons to take, and so much life to live. I spent my youthful years as a jazz singer, and it was another of life's twists and turns that, under the guidance of Alice and Strybjörn Lindedal, I began to train for roles in musical theatre, operetta and opera – a career path that found me at Wigmore Hall in 1962.

There were many twists and turns in those years – and the occasional bump on the road! Success in the field of singing depends on so many things – talent and ability, definitely, but training, endurance, the ability to do well in auditions, and the willingness to learn and keep on learning all play a huge part. So does luck, or fate, or chance, or however else one can describe being in the right place at just the right time.

It seemed the planets were in alignment for me, as during the next eight years I performed in Zurich with a jazz band, had a role in *My Fair Lady* for a year in Gothenburg, and won a scholarship to study in London – where I first heard Jon sing. I worked in the theatre, and in musical theatre and operetta in those years, and won a scholarship awarded by Sweden's leading company which entailed a five-year touring contract.

In another of those twists and turns, I found myself being invited to tour Russia for a month. If that were not surprising enough – the Berlin Wall was still in existence, and the East still hostile and suspicious of the West – the fact that they wanted to hear 'decadent' jazz was mind-boggling!

Then it was off to Austria for the lead role in *The Gypsy Princess*, and, later, the final twist and turn of the fateful audition for *The Merry Widow* in Kiel.

Love at first sight? Perhaps, but also something stronger and more valuable, able to stand the tests of long separations, the endless travelling of professional singing careers, and the arrival of a beloved child.

Chapter Two

The only thing better than singing is more singing.
Ella Fitzgerald

Gothenburg, 1940 – 48

I used to be Monica Brynnel.

I feel as though I was born knowing that I had to prove how much better I was than the boys. As a child I preferred playing with boys as it gave me the opportunity to show off but I was smart enough to disappear if a football appeared. When it came to climbing the roofs of the houses in our neighbourhood in Gothenburg, I was the first to reach the top.

My mother, Greta Viola Brandt, was – and still is – a mystery to me. I can honestly say that, even today, I'm not quite sure who she is. She was born in 1909 into a very musical family. Her great-grandfather, Johann Christoph Heussermann, created and introduced Kasper to Sweden. Kasper became one of the most popular 'talking doll' theatre icons in the mid-1800s and is immortalised in a statue in Stockholm.

Greta had two sisters and one brother. Her brother Bernhard was conducting at the age of four and was the youngest conductor in the world until he died of tuberculosis when he was eight years old. The remaining three children were all taught to play string instruments and sing classical repertoire. They performed together as 'Brandtska Solist Familjen'.

Monique's Solo

My grandparents, Bernhardina and Bertholdy Brandt, toured, performing classical concerts. They were entrepreneurs and were amongst the first people to show moving pictures in Sweden. Bernhardina was a powerful woman and was the driving force behind their professional lives. Bertholdy was just a 'spillevink' who loved women, wine and music.

Brandtska Solist Familjen: Bertholdy, Bernhardina, Bernhard (aged three) with accompanying violinist at left, 1903

Bernhardina was a handsome woman, strong, and intelligent, and I identified with her, much more than with my own mother. She was also wealthy but lacked business acumen. Her pride led her to make an unfortunate error of judgement.

The family lived in the Shire of Bastad. In the 1930s the Shire was having financial problems and approached Bernhardina with an offer to sell her the coastline of Bastad for 5 cents per square metre. Insulted, she refused, believing they thought that because she was a woman she would be foolish enough to buy miles of sand. Bastad and its surroundings has since become the Riviera of Sweden.

The family was well known to Swedish cinema-goers. Author and Nobel Laureate Harry Martinsson wrote in his memoirs about an episode in his youth when he went to see his first film.

> In the box office there was a lady with a fur thrown over her shoulders and her fingers covered with huge rings. She came across as very strong and frightening, with ice cold eyes staring at you as if trying to see how much money you had in your pocket.
>
> When she handed me the ticket, she was decidedly unfriendly.
>
> There was a pause in the middle of the film, where the box office lady, Bernhardina, came in with a harp, joined by the manager, bringing a violin and two young adults, also with violins, and together they entertained the audience with fifteen minutes of classical music.

Greta was an introvert and gave the impression of being sweet and shy, but in fact she was very smart. She was the dominant one in my parents' marriage. Although smart, she seemed devoid of feelings. She was a constantly smiling doll who never displayed any emotions.

When Greta was four, she and her sisters were sent away to a foster home, where they remained until Greta was twelve. It must have been devastating to be taken away from her parents at such a young age. Fortunately the foster couple who looked after them were caring and wonderful people, and she often spoke of how fond she was of them.

She never showed any anger or sadness, and rarely showed any happiness or warmth. I cannot remember ever having felt her arms around me when I was a child, nor that she told me that she loved me. I sometimes wonder whether, on the day she married my father and locked away her cello in a wardrobe, she also locked away her feelings.

I wish I could recall my life as a newborn baby for at that moment at least she would have held me in her arms.

Monique, aged two

I was born during World War II and I imagine the atmosphere was tense around the time of my mother's pregnancy. Although Sweden took a neutral stance with Ireland, Portugal, Spain, Andorra, Liechentein, Vatican City and Switzerland, I am aware that there is a feeling of shame in Sweden about our role in the war. Sweden's pre-war economy was in a terrible state. Despite Sweden's neutrality, it supplied iron ore to Germany and also allowed Germany to use its railway during the Russian invasion. My mother joined a protest at the railway station.

At the same time Sweden became a refuge for anti-fascist and Jewish refugees from all over the region. In 1943, following an order to deport Denmark's Jewish population to concentration camps, nearly all of Denmark's 8000 Jews were brought to safety in Sweden. Sweden also provided a safe haven to Jews from Norway.

Albin Hansson, then Swedish Prime Minister, stated on 1 September 1939:

> Friendly with all nations and strongly linked to our neighbours, we look on no one as our enemy. There is no place in the thoughts of our people for aggression against any other country, and we note with gratitude the assurance from others that they have no wish to disturb our peace, our freedom, or our independence. The strengthening of our defence preparations serves merely to underline our fixed determination to keep our country outside the conflicts that may erupt amongst others and, during such conflicts, to safeguard the existence of our people.

It is clear he knew war was coming. The atmosphere around that time was tense, particularly as there were many Nazi sympathizers in Sweden.

In 1944 and 1945, Sweden allowed the Allied forces to use Swedish airports, attempting to balance their neutrality and recognizing that the Allies had won the war.

After the war Sweden managed to recover economically. The cuisine was fairly primitive, the basic foods being potatoes and apples. There were no exotic foods like bananas and oranges. Tea was totally unimportant to the Swedes but when England sent a ship with coffee everyone was very excited.

Jon's and my backgrounds were similar in several ways. There was some shame attached to both cultures – for different reasons – that perhaps led to a chip on the shoulder. Many Swedes were ashamed of their role in the war and many Australians were ashamed of their convict background and felt patronized by the British. Both of us were born into families with Christian backgrounds and no doubt were influenced by the music we were exposed to at school and at home.

Most photos of the Brynnel family show my father Erik, holding one of us children tightly to his chest or firmly by one of our hands.

Erik was in the police force and was possibly more a danger to the female population than a protector. He was a strikingly handsome man, particularly in his uniform. He had a charming, fun side to his personality and an excellent voice. When he felt really happy, he sometimes took up a violin and produced some music that would really stun us all. Unfortunately there was a hidden dark side to Erik, one that threw a heavy shadow over his three children – my older brother Lasse, my younger sister Rose Marie, and of course, myself.

Erik had been a polite, well-educated young man from a very strict, religious, middle-class family when he entered the police force in the mid-1930s. This was a time when people didn't talk openly about homosexuality. One night, when he and his colleagues at the police station were playing cards to keep themselves awake, one of the men happened to mention that the Chief Commander of the Swedish Police Force was homosexual.

Erik was not a person who indulged in gossip about other people's personal lives but, on another occasion while playing cards with a different group of policemen, he mentioned the man's preferences. A few days later he was interrogated by officials from Stockholm, who wanted to know the source of his information. In spite of warnings that he would be punished in different ways if he didn't give them the details they wanted, Erik refused to reveal his source. Consequently he stayed a police constable for the rest of his professional life, and his monthly income stayed the same as it had been from the very first day he entered the Force.

He believed that he was the winner because he did not betray the man who told him. We believed that not only was he the loser, but the whole family was punished since he began to use alcohol to help him cope. Some people are happy and funny when they drink, but this was not so with Erik.

It was like having a father with two personalities – a Jekyll and Hyde. On weekends we kids had nothing to be afraid of or hide from. Weekdays on the other hand could be very, very scary. If he was drunk, he was mean and violent, swearing and physically abusing us, and we never knew when he would be drunk.

We had a good education, and a solid roof over our heads, but we were starved of parental love and support. How did this affect us? I don't know. What I do know is that music became the reason for living for all three of us. We did not hear music often at home

Music and Love

but were born with music in our genes. Lasse's passion was jazz, and playing the drums gave him the opportunity to get out some of his pent-up feelings. Rose Marie loved folk music and this became her profession. I loved everything from jazz to opera. At the same time we learnt to value silence as it soothed us and helped us escape from the pain of listening to the screaming abuse from Erik.

Erik Brynnel, at right, pictured with a friend, Gothenburg, 1935

My real life began one dark December night in 1946 at a Christmas celebration for the children of the members of the police force. It was held in a hall at Valand in Gothenburg.

Monique's Solo

There was a 'before' and 'after' to this event. The 'before' was terrifying. I had no idea that Greta had planned for me to have my stage debut that evening. She took my hand and suddenly I found myself at the end of the big hall where the stairs led up to the stage. We walked up the stairs and across the stage where she left me in front of the microphone. She looked down at me, said, 'Just smile!' and then left. I remember staring at her back as she walked away, stunned that this person I trusted had just walked away and left me in front of a crowd of people.

I have no idea what I sang. I came to my senses at the sound of the applause, and that was the moment the seed was planted. I knew what I wanted to do. The 'after' was the beginning of becoming aware of a new part of myself, who I was, and the importance of music for my soul.

In 1948, when I was eight years old we moved to Pixbo, a small village beside two beautiful lakes, about twenty minutes by train from Gothenburg. There were only about fifty houses and everybody knew each other. It was a very happy time for me.

I joined the 'Frisksportarklubben', a club for young people who were interested in sport. I liked to watch the sport even though I wasn't particularly interested in participating.

One beautiful summer day, I was watching some men practicing discus throwing and, in my enthusiasm must have gone too close to the action. Five minutes later I woke up, flat on the ground with people all around me. I had been hit on the head by a discus. My skull was fractured and I was taken to the children's hospital at Sahlgrenska. I remember feeling fine, no pain or blood, but I couldn't talk.

I spent five weeks isolated in a glass chamber in the corner of a big room containing about ten other sick children. Something happened which I find difficult to describe, but it made a big impression on me. I was lying on my back when suddenly an adult female voice spoke to me and it seemed to come from inside my head. She said, 'Monica, one of the children is going to ask you for your name. You have to be able to say Monica Brynnel. Start practicing right now!' I moved my lips and tongue and mumbled 'Mo...oo...mon...'. At this stage one of the children, a young girl, got out of her bed, dressed and walked to the door at the end of the big room. She was stopped by a nurse, who bent down and spoke to her. The girl turned around and walked back to the glass chamber, opened the door and said, 'I'm going home today and would like to write to you. What's your name?'

'Mm-m-moni-cahhhh...B..b..brynnel.'

I COULD SPEAK! I was healed.

Sixty years after this incident, I received an email from a man who grew up in Pixbo, and has been living in the United States since the mid-1950s. He had been standing next to me on that very day the discus landed on my head. After some correspondence back and forth between us, he wrote:

> 18 September 2008
>
> Hello Monica,
> Now comes the follow up to part one of your letter. It was such a terrible accident and I am pleased we can talk about it now. I was afraid that you had shut it out of your mind and did not want to, or did not feel like, talking about it.
> And I wondered if maybe you had blacked out on the period just before and after the accident as so often happens to people in accidents. It was such an extreme careless action, to throw a discus into a field full of people.
> I was standing next to you when it happened. There was a thump sound, no, rather a clonk sound. I turned to you and saw your eyeballs roll around in their sockets and I saw nothing but the whites of your eyes. I've never seen that before, and not since, and it was very scary. I believe I was the only one that stood this close to you and saw what your eyes did. Then you went down like the KO victim you were.
> I am blacking out on what followed. Was your brother there? Did we call your parents? Did the ambulance come?
> As awful as the accident was and such bad luck you had to stand right there, in that spot, I cannot help but think what consequences would have been had the discus hit with the steel rimmed edge rather than hitting with the flat area.
> Whenever I watch a track-and-field event on TV, like the Olympics, I always scan the field to make sure nobody is there when they throw the discus, javelin or hammer-throw. So my mind has been programmed.

    I hope this does not wear you down or depress you, but please let me know, if it does. Maybe because I stood so close to you and saw the effect the blow had on your body I have always taken a interest in what happened to you, your singing and your life. I always asked our friends whenever I was back in Pixbo. I learned that you were singing for Malte Johnsson. Years went by and Arne in Molndal sent me clippings about your singing at the Opera House in Sydney. What a building! Must be uplifting for the soul and spirit to enter and perform in such a building!

    Let's continue, when you feel like it, at a later time.

Hugs,

Figg

    No, my brother was not there and no-one rang my parents and there was no ambulance. Someone took me home on the back of a bike. My mother was alone at home and unable to leave my little sister, so she called my Aunt Marta. She was a very kind woman and a trained nurse. She came in a taxi as quickly as she could, and brought me to the hospital.

Chapter Three

That is the difference between good teachers and great teachers: good teachers make the best of a pupil's means; great teachers foresee a pupil's ends.
Maria Callas

Alice and Styrbjörn Lindedal

The excitement of my first stage experience, smiling and singing my heart out at that unforgettable Christmas celebration in 1946, has never left me. I had never any doubt about what I wanted to do. I wanted to sing.

Meanwhile, my mother demanded that I spend four years studying typing and shorthand at Practiska Mellan Skolan. When I asked her why, she explained that I needed something to fall back on if things didn't work out. I thought she was out of her mind. I had absolutely no doubt that things would work out. They did, but it took several years for this to happen.

One resident of Pixbo, Bo Cullberg, was a very unusual man. He established the sporting club (Frisksportarklubben) where we could engage in any sport of our choice. We could also make music, which of course was my interest. Bo set up a studio where we could rehearse and record whatever music we liked. This happened to be mostly jazz and 1950s repertoire.

When I was about twelve, I had a large enough repertoire to enter competitions and I was lucky enough to win them. There was a very popular program host on Swedish radio, Lennart Hyland, who later became even more famous as a television host. He invited me to perform on one of his programs. That was the beginning of the professional stage of my life.

Monique, aged 12, singing competition

I started to tour Sweden as a jazz singer with the Ken Lains band. Looking back, if I had a fourteen-year-old daughter wanting to tour

Music and Love

the country with six men I would have said 'No!' I was very lucky that the six musicians treated me like their daughter and became my guardians. They helped to make this a very happy chapter in my life.

For the first six years of my schooling I excelled, encouraged by my teacher, Nils Rasin. My parents, on the other hand, hardly ever opened my report card.

Monique, aged 14, with Ken Lains' Orchestra, Gothenburg, 1953

At the age of twelve, according to my mother's wishes, I was to commence at Praktiska Mellanskolan, a secretarial college. My Uncle Gustaf, headmaster of a school in Stockholm, was friendly with the headmaster at PRAM. Uncle Gustaf proudly told him that his niece, a top student, was enrolled at his school.

By this stage I had lost all interest in studying. At the end of the term as I sat in the examination room scanning the shorthand exam paper, I realized, too late, that shorthand requires practice. In a very short space of time after the examiner had read out the article we were to write down, he received my exam paper on his desk. He congratulated me and announced he had never had a student able to finish the task so fast. No wonder, as I hadn't written a single word.

If you had told me at this time of my life that God was a woman and asked me for her name, I would have replied without hesitation, Ella Fitzgerald! I admired her more than any other singer in the world. The first time I heard her sing was at the Concert Hall in Gothenburg in the mid-1950s, where she performed with Count Basie. Her eyesight was poor, and she needed to be led onto the stage but when she opened her mouth, and I heard her voice, I was in heaven!

I sang my entire repertoire in English, unusual at that time in Sweden. (This was a long time before ABBA!) When I was fifteen, HMV wanted to sign me up and so I arranged a meeting with them at their office in Stockholm. When asked about the titles of the songs I would be interested in for the first recording, I gave them 'Sunny Side of the Street', and 'Basin Street Blues'. They were happy with the choices but wanted me to sing Swedish lyrics.

'No, that's not necessary! I only sing in English!' I replied.

Then the manager took my hand and showed me around their premises, pointing at all the pictures of their Swedish stars. He asked

'Do you really think they would have been famous if they had sung in English?'

I replied, 'Well, that's their bad luck.'

Full of fifteen-year-old arrogance, I picked up my bag and flounced out of the door. Nothing in the world would have made me sing jazz in Swedish and a couple of years later, they changed their tune.

I looked forward to a life totally dedicated to a singing career. What I didn't know was that my life was about to have a dramatic change of direction. Alice Sterner, an operetta diva and wife of Styrbjörn Lindedal, chief conductor and soon to be Intendant of

Stora Teatern in Gothenburg, lived not very far from our house in Pixbo. We happened to be in the village shop at the same time one day, and the owner introduced me to Alice as a young singer. I was eighteen at the time.

Alice was immediately interested and curious about my voice, and invited me to come to her place to sing for her. She was not impressed with my choice of music, but did not mention that to me at the time. This meeting was to change my life.

After I sang for them, Alice suggested that not only should I change my name to Monique, but I should also begin to take my singing seriously. I moved in with Alice and Styrbjörn and their cuddly Airedale dog Chimmy in the autumn of 1958.

I needed an income and so took a job as the secretary of the new director of Pixbo Pals, a company owned by Bo Cullberg, the founder of the Frisksportarklubben. Every day I had two singing lessons with Alice, one during my lunch break and the other straight after work.

The change of genre meant it was time to say goodbye to the Ken Lains band. The new singing adventure was so stimulating that, strangely enough, I didn't feel any sadness in closing this chapter.

As well as singing lessons, Alice and Styrbjörn also encouraged me to take dancing lessons with the choreographer at Stora Teatern. This was an embarrassing experience. I had no ballet experience or knowledge and yet was expected to take part in the warm-up of the ballet at the Opera House.

Alice and Styrbjörn also introduced me to a new dimension of music – the classical world. Alice wanted me to listen to the very best, and gave me a recording of Dame Joan Sutherland. I was totally overwhelmed. What a voice. What a technique. Who was she? I felt ashamed that I knew nothing about her.

Alice, Styrbjörn and I would have laughed if someone had told us that not only was I to meet her, but that she was to become a good friend. I was also going to perform and record with this amazing person and even take over a part from her, walking on stage in her costumes.

This really did happen, in 1983. (Dreams really do come true!) Before that, Joan and I performed together in *Die Fledermaus* in 1982, which was recorded and shown on the ABC. The ABC received 35000 requests for the program after the performance.

In 1984, the Australian Opera staged *The Merry Widow* in the Sydney Opera House to celebrate Joan Sutherland's presence in Australia. Joan was Hanna Glawari; new costumes were made, new arias were added and the finale was altered to suit her voice and presence.

Unfortunately, Joan had to leave the production after several performances as she had commitments in Chicago. I was asked to take over the part. This was a most exciting experience: she was my idol and it felt like the most unbelievable honour to be asked to take over her role.

The costumes had been designed for Dame Joan and were more in the line of classic opera costumes. New costumes made to measure for me followed that classical design. She looked wonderful in them but I didn't. It didn't matter – I was in heaven singing the role I had sung hundreds of times before and stepping out on stage in Sydney Opera House in Joan's own hats and using her props. There is a video on You Tube of me singing the entrance song from this production.

But this was to be many years in the future. I was still a teenager in Pixbo.

I enjoyed the three years I spent working at an office. The office was only five minutes' walk from where I lived so I woke at 7.50 am, threw some clothes over my pyjamas and ran to work to arrive at 8.00. On arrival, I used the office bathroom to shower and dress, the office kitchen to prepare some breakfast and, if I was lucky, also had time for another snooze at my office desk. The boss usually arrived at 9.00 am and my colleagues alerted me if the boss was inconsiderate enough to turn up early.

The Merry Widow, Sydney, 1984, wearing Dame Joan Sutherland's hat!

Alice and Styrbjörn had made it very clear that if I really wanted a singing career, I had to be serious and forget about running around with boys. I knew Alice really meant it, and I didn't want to disappoint her, or do anything that might stop her from believing in me. I desperately longed to be on the stage again, and I knew that this was unlikely to happen if I became distracted. But I fell in love.

One beautiful summer weekend I joined a couple of girlfriends at the beach in Langedrag, Gothenburg, for a swim and sunbathing. Tumba, a well-known sporting icon in Sweden, and his brother,

Nisse, happened to be there, teaching people to water-ski. This was a sport unknown in Scandinavia at that time.

Nisse and Tumba asked if I would be interested in having a go. Of course I was, but did not want to have my first experience with hundreds of people watching. So I told them I knew how to water-ski but wasn't really keen right there and then. Unfortunately, they took this as my acceptance. Before I knew what was happening I was sitting on a wooden bridge with skis stuck to my feet, and my hands holding on to a rope.

Off we went. I actually managed to stand up on the skis and this convinced the guys that I was accustomed to water-skiing. The speeding boat took me straight out into the scary-looking sea of Skagerack. After about ten minutes, the guys decided the fun was over and turned the boat quickly to head for land. It was a bit too quick and I fell. I truly thought these were my last seconds alive. Land was so far away and I was sure I would never reach it again. The guys turned the boat around, picked up the skis and told me to jump aboard. That proved to be impossible. They decided that I should try to get up on the skis again. Just getting them on my feet while I tried to keep my head above water was like running a marathon. When I succeeded on the third attempt the relief was overwhelming. My legs were shaking not just from stress but the extraordinary 'workout'.

Nisse was more than impressed with my exhibition and invited me out. After a short courtship we became engaged. When I introduced Nisse to my parents, my Dad took him aside and whispered in his ear, 'You can find something much better!' Nisse was very upset on my behalf and wanted to punch my father. When Nisse told me what had been said, I understood the reason for my father's comment. It was not that my father didn't like me: it was his way of trying to get rid of Nisse. His action would of course have been applauded by Alice and Styrbjörn.

My relationship with Nisse did not affect my preparation for a future as a singer. Nisse lived in Stockholm and so we didn't see each other on a daily basis. The engagement lasted about two years. Although the engagement ended, I have remained close to his family ever since.

One day, walking through Stockholm while filling in time before lunch with Nisse, a one-armed photographer approached me and asked whether I would allow him to take some snapshots of me. I was a normal, easily impressed teenager and enjoyed posing in front of hundreds of people in the centre of the city. He gave me his card and told me he was from Austria. He also told me he was travelling around Scandinavia for a German magazine, putting together a folder of 'nice-looking Viking girls'. He offered to show me what he had already done. He said he was staying in a hotel nearby, and I had another half-hour to fill in. We were in the centre of Stockholm, it was the middle of the day and the man only had one arm. Not thinking there was any risk, I went with him to see the photographs.

In his room was a big table full of fantastic photos of lovely looking girls. While I was admiring them, I suddenly smelt something strange, and realized it was ether. I turned around and saw the one-armed man coming towards me with a big cotton ball in his only hand. As I rushed to the door, which was fortunately unlocked, I heard him calling out that he wanted to wash off the black spot I had on my neck. I ran and ran and ran!

This incident has stayed in my mind all these years because I am ashamed now that I did not go to the police. Perhaps I might have saved other women from being kidnapped and sent to southern parts of Europe as sex slaves. (At the time, I was not aware of things like this happening, as it was never mentioned in the media in the 1950s.) I didn't want anyone to know how foolish I had been. Needless to say, I had no black spot on my neck. It is chilling to think that the appeal of being photographed could have had such disastrous consequences.

After one year's study, I received an offer to sing with 'Fredrik's Glade Show'. This was a group of musicians who normally worked with Svend Asmundsen, a famous violinist from Denmark. I was very nervous when asking Alice and Styrbjörn what they thought about me going back to my jazz for a month. They both smiled, and looked really happy. I couldn't believe it. I almost lost my breath. Could it be that they both actually liked Svend Asmundsen?

I flew to Copenhagen for one week's rehearsal with the band before we were to leave for Zurich. We planned to spend three weeks performing in a club and were also booked for a guest appearance on television.

The musicians were all very nice and caring but at our first meeting, to my dismay and distress, I didn't understand one word they said. They spoke Danish! This should not have been a surprise, but strangely enough, it was. I was too embarrassed to let them know that I didn't have a clue what they were saying, and instead tried to sing as well as I possibly could, so maybe they wouldn't notice. Panic-stricken, I decided I would have to tell them the truth the next day, and cancel the engagement. It never occurred to me that I could have overcome the problem by suggesting we spoke English.

The next morning, shaking, I walked into the studio ready to deliver the bombshell. But miracles do happen. Suddenly, to my amazement I found I understood what they were saying – not every word, but the message was clear enough. It was as if my brain had needed twenty-four hours to adjust to the melody of the Danish language. It felt wonderful and such a relief.

We were ready to leave for Zurich. There were two girls in the show, Jeanette, a dancer and me. Jeanette was one year younger, and I was asked to look after her since she seemed sweet and innocent. Don't you believe it! The instant the door to our room in the hotel closed she underwent a personality change. She was the boss. I learned a lot about how women can manipulate men through watching Jeanette in action.

The show went well and I really enjoyed my time in Zurich. On the day we did the television show, I happened to be about half an hour too early in the studio. I found my way into the make-up room and my eyes rested on a can of hair spray of what I thought to be blonde colouring. I had never been blonde so gave myself a couple of blonde shots to my hair. While I was doing this, the musicians arrived. They took one look at me and screamed, 'Get that "effing" stuff out of your hair or forget about the recording!'

Singing lesson: Monique with teacher and mentor
Alice Sterner, 1961

I couldn't understand their reaction until I looked in the mirror. The spray was grey, not blonde – I thought I was looking at my grandmother! I desperately worked on removing the grey from my hair before the filming, scared that I would lose my voice in my panic. Fortunately my attempts were successful and my voice remained true.

The engagement in Zurich was a 'one off' and I really did enjoy most of the time in beautiful Switzerland. Three weeks went by quickly, and before I knew it I was back in Pixbo and the 'old routine'.

Chapter Four

Don't take yourself too seriously. Take art seriously.

My Fair Lady... and off to London

One day, out of the blue, Alice announced that it was time to start looking for a good audition piece for *My Fair Lady*. She and Styrbjörn thought it was time for me to try my feet on the professional musical stage, and this was a perfect role for me to begin my career. A new production was planned for the Circus Theatre in Gothenburg, starring Harriet Forsell and the great Swedish male star Jarl Kulle as Professor Higgins. We had one month to prepare for the audition, a month during which I hardly slept.

I remember nothing about the audition, but the rehearsals were great fun. I was offered the role of one of the three servant

Monique rehearsing *My Fair Lady* with Lauritz Falk, Gothenburg, 1961

girls, which I naturally accepted. I think Eliza is one of the greatest roles for a female artist. There is the opportunity to show the whole palette of emotions – fun, anger, love, desperation, and innocence. I was given that opportunity when I was selected as the understudy for Eliza. Extraordinary, since I had no acting experience and in fact had never uttered a spoken word on stage. *Gott sei Dank,* Harriet Forsell stayed healthy through the whole run of the show. I would have run for my life if she had been unable to perform and I had been expected to save the performance.

There is one incident I recall clearly. It happened on the night of the dress rehearsal. Jarl Kulle had his dressing room next to ours and I knocked on his door. There was no answer so I knocked again. A voice bellowed, 'Who is it?'

The bellow was so loud it could have been heard in the street. I wanted to run but was frozen to the ground. After a moment, Kulle appeared at the door and barked,

'What do you want?'

'Just your autograph, please', I whispered.

'NEVER, NEVER DISTURB ME AGAIN BEFORE A PERFORMANCE! DO YOU UNDERSTAND?'

I certainly did. I wonder what the reaction would have been if he had arrived one night to be told he was to share the stage with me, a total amateur, playing Eliza.

During *My Fair Lady* I fell in love with the musical stage. I was unhappy when the show finished after a year of sold-out performances. The show had to finish because of other contract agreements of the principals. Life became unbelievably boring, despite daily singing lessons. I wanted to be on stage.

Alice and Styrbjörn didn't just help me with the development of my voice. They also introduced me to the world of classical music. I saw *Gypsy Princess* at Stora Teatern, with Styrbjörn conducting. This was my first exposure to the world of operetta. As I sat in the first row in the stalls, I thought, *Styrbjörn and Alice are mad. How can they imagine that I could go on stage and perform operetta?* The thought was terrifying.

Alice decided my voice needed a final polishing and according to her the best person to do so was her old friend and colleague Mme Triguez, in London. She specialized in working with the top register and this was the part of my voice that I'd never really liked using. Styrbjörn enquired about a scholarship for me. He was quite sure that I would get it, so he made a booking for me on a ship sailing for England.

Weeks and months passed by and there was no response from the scholarship administrators. Styrbjörn was quite annoyed, and thought it was particularly rude that the people in charge of the scholarship didn't have the manners to contact him one way or the other. Two days before I was due to leave, he announced in frustration that he was going to cancel the ticket the next day.

I was devastated. I didn't know what to do with myself. In desperation I began to clean the house. As I was dusting the back of one of the bookcases by the front door, a white envelope fell to the floor. I picked it up and was about to put it back on the shelf when I noticed my name written on the front, so I opened it. To my horror, it was a letter advising that 'S.Kr.5,000 is given to Miss Monica Brynnel. Please acknowledge...' before a certain date, well past. Fortunately, everyone knew Styrbjörn and to my great relief I was still able to accept the scholarship.

I have never solved the mystery of how the letter ended up behind the books in the hall. The post was always delivered by the postman through a slit in the front door. Perhaps Gunnar, a young relative of Alice's who had visited us earlier, had seen the letter lying on the floor inside the front door, picked it up and put it on the bookshelf.

I was jumping up and down with excitement. My cases were packed and I was off to London.

Chapter Five

*Embrace and practice Art as a way of unveiling
the truth of our deep creative self.*

Money, money, money

I felt as though I was walking on clouds as I waved farewell to Alice, Styrbjörn, and Rose Marie from the deck of the ship. A trip to London felt so overwhelmingly adventurous and exciting as I had never been in England before.

The ship arrived at Harwich the following morning and I took the train to London. I was met by Kjerstin Svensson, the lovely director of the hostel. Immediately, I was struck down by a very nasty case of flu and ended up spending the first week in London in bed. So much for having a great time!

During this first week in the hostel I learnt a most important ritual to be observed when living in England. When making tea, the water must be boiling when you pour it over the leaves. As I have never been a tea drinker I didn't really care.

The first lesson with Mme Triguez was difficult. Still suffering from the flu, I was not able to really show her my voice. I liked her immediately, both as a teacher and a person and she invited me to address her as Billy. Like Alice, Billy didn't like my name and changed it to Karen. I was becoming completely confused. I couldn't understand what was wrong with Monica. Was I Monica, Monique or Karen? I found it ridiculous.

Billy was teaching in the studios at Wigmore Hall and, of course, this is where I had the pleasure of hearing the voice of the tenor whose owner was to change my life.

My three months in London was disappointing. I don't think I have ever felt so lonely. I knew no one except the people at the hostel and Billy. I remember going twice to see a film and once to see a musical. In spite of living like a hermit, the money just disappeared. It even worried Alice and Styrbjörn, until we all realized the costs for the lessons were more than double the estimated sum, as I ended up having five lessons a week instead of the planned two lessons.

Billy focused the coaching on my upper register as this was her specialty. She was a high soprano with coloratura herself. We became very close and one day she told me about her short career. When she completed her singing education in Italy, she auditioned at La Scala, Milan, and was given a contract straight away as a leading soprano, which is unheard of. One can easily imagine her tension as she prepared for her debut. During her first aria on opening night she realized that she had sung one bar incorrectly and, in horror, just stopped singing. As if in a dream she walked forward and asked the conductor to start again from the beginning, which he did. The La Scala audiences are renowned for either greeting performances with 'Brava' or 'Buhhhh", with nothing in between. There are many people paid to produce the 'Brava' 'or 'Buhhh' sounds. Poor Billy. At that moment she was aware that if she didn't sing this particular aria better than it has ever been sung at La Scala, she was about to be drowned out by the 'Buhhhs' from the audience.

She sang the aria beautifully and received a huge 'Brava'. It was a great success but she cancelled her contract and never went on stage again. She had lost her confidence completely.

Naturally Billy could not give me lessons without payment and my situation was becoming dire. It was disheartening to receive a letter from Styrbjörn, where he suggested I was unaware of my good fortune.

>Styrbjörn Lindedal
>
>Stora Teatern
>
>Gothenburg
>
>26 July 1962

Dear Monique,

I am sitting here by myself composing a letter to you. I am back in town as the opera opened this week. Alice is having another week's rest in Asa. Alice told me she received a long – AND EXPENSIVE – telegram from you that you are planning a trip to Austria – or was it Switzerland! It's hard to understand your letters sometimes.

I'd like to point out that getting a large Scholarship as you just have, gives you a big responsibility. As you were chosen purely on my recommendation I also feel responsible. A Scholarship of this magnitude would last at least 6 months, if not longer, for a focused and serious student.

I'm wondering if you really understand the importance of the advantage that you've been given. Obviously I have no knowledge of how much effort you've put into your studies or how much you have progressed. Whatever happens – a scholarship is not meant to be wasted on some holiday trip – as a journey to Austria would be.

You've mentioned that you've worked out that you would have no money left by the end of August – if not earlier! You would then come home with two empty hands. And – then what?! Have you ever thought about what you are going to do when you get back? You will of course do auditions, but unfortunately it's the wrong time of the year for most Opera Houses and you would have to show something extraordinary to even be considered. You could of course get office work again – but is that what you want?

Many people in the theatre world are now aware of you and expecting you to deliver something sensational. You remember what I told you about Brahms? 'Nothing is as hard as to live up to expectations!"

You are probably not very happy getting this letter with all my remarks. I just had to write to you as I would be really sad if you didn't live up to the expectations when you get back. No human being can do the impossible, but one can always try one's best and when doing so – the impossible might happen!

Maybe I'm judging your situation wrongly; maybe my worries are unnecessary. I really hope so! Be very wise when making plans. Remember you've got a long future ahead of you and you are not a baby any longer, so please, don't make any childish decision. The road you've chosen is hard and full of hardship – not a child's play. It's one thing to have fun; the career has to be taken seriously. You don't want to have a future in a choir – or?

So – have a long and serious thought about your future. At the end it's up to you to decide – I have only sent you my thoughts about this. You and your future are very precious to both Alice and I, and we know you're an intelligent young girl even if you're 'up in the clouds' sometimes. Nothing wrong with that!

All my love to Billy and yourself.

Always your 'Tuktomaster' and friend,

Styrbjörn

Imagine how I felt reading this letter from someone who had been, and still was, a deeply valued mentor and supporter.

Chapter Six

Opera is for a lifetime, not just a minute.
Dame Kiri Te Kanawa

Back to Sweden

Getting back to Sweden turned out to be quite an adventure. Billy insisted that I come with her to Seefeld in Austria where she was going to spend her usual three weeks' annual holiday. En route we were to stop in Munich so I could audition for one of the best agencies in Germany. The lack of funds seemed to be an insurmountable problem, then I received a letter from my aunt containing a cheque for about S.Kr.500, on the understanding that I would pay it back at a later date.

The audition went really well; they liked me and asked me to return to Germany as soon as possible, and they would be very happy to organize auditions for me in different opera houses.

I danced out of the studio into the arms of Billy, who was anxiously waiting outside to hear how the audition went. I felt I was ready to take on the world, and was now eagerly looking forward to showing Alice and Styrbjörn the result of my three months in London.

When we reached the hotel in Seefeld, the daily singing routine became the same as in London, except we were allowed to use the organ in the main church of Seefeld. As in many churches,

Monique's Solo

the acoustics were more than perfect. I didn't even mind using my dreaded top register.

As most singers know, it is important to stop singing before the voice gets tired. A pianist or violinist can keep practicing for hours but a singer should not do so. If you do, there is no voice left next day, and all you can do is keep quiet until the poor vocal cords have recovered from the abuse.

So I had free time to spend with my coach after we finished the usual routine of one hour in the morning and one in the afternoon. The rest of the day was spent going for walks, enjoying the fantastic countryside, and reading.

The three weeks went extremely fast, and it was soon time for me to take the train back to Sweden after an emotional farewell with Billy.

I had contacted Jeanette, the young dancer I worked with in Zurich, telling her I would have a couple of hours between trains in Copenhagen, where she lived. Jeanette picked me up in her open-top car and we sped through the centre of Copenhagen to her apartment. She insisted that I stay at least a couple of days with her.

When she opened the door to the apartment I was knocked over by a shocking smell. I realized what it was when I saw a monkey running around inside. I planned to tell her that I would not be staying longer than one day, as the smell was overwhelming, but something happened to change my mind.

Jeanette was a busy model with a good reputation. When she heard about my financial situation, she insisted I accompany her to a fashion show followed by the filming of an advertisement inside an aeroplane. I enjoyed the filming in the plane, and was delighted to be earning some much-needed cash. The director of the film crew told us that they needed a girl with nice legs for another advertisement. He explained that they would only film from the waist down. I thought this was a great opportunity. If I was successful, nobody would know that it was me. I stood in a row of six other women while the director checked us out. Much to my amazement, I got the job. It turned out to be a full body shot and not just my legs, so my wish to remain anonymous was not fulfilled.

However, in less than six hours, I had earned more than I had been paid at the office for a month's work. I got used to the monkey smell, and stayed a couple more days with my smart girlfriend Jeanette.

It was lovely to be back in Gothenburg, even though I got the feeling that Alice when she heard me singing, didn't think much of Billy's coaching. This made me a bit sad and confused.

It was time to make my debut in Stockholm, and a few weeks later I set off to auditions that had been arranged. On 17 November 1962, I signed four contracts!

All my auditions had been successful. I was engaged to make my debut on the musical stage at Oscars Teatern as one of the leads in a new English musical *Lock Up Your Daughters*.

I was also signed up for the December show at Hamburger Bors with Stig Grybe and Tor Isedal and this was to be great fun. On top of that I was going to be introduced for the first time on Swedish television in a special musical Christmas celebration. I was very nervous as I had no experience of television. The fourth contract was signed in the back of a taxi! An agent from Decca had found out about me and came rushing to the audition at Oscars Teatern. He jumped in the car that was taking me to my next audition, and wanted my signature there and then. He would not listen when I asked him to wait and insisted I make up my mind immediately. Regrettably, I signed away five years of my recording life.

I stayed with my mother's Uncle Bernhard and his wife Helga in Stockholm and was well looked after. They made me feel very comfortable and at home.

I was also comfortable in the show at Hamburger Bors. It was truly enjoyable and there was no pressure. We were even encouraged to clown around on stage. The pressure started during the rehearsals at Oscars Teatern. I was the only beginner amongst a cast of well-known names in the Swedish theatre world. In the 1960s it was expected that performers spoke a kind of BBC version of Swedish, refined and bearing no trace of a regional accent. Nothing else was accepted. This type of Swedish is very close to Stockholmska. I spoke Goteborgska. One of Sweden's best actresses, Renée Björling, stepped in and helped me to get rid of my Goteborgska Swedish.

At this time there was a tradition in Sweden of inviting newspaper critics to attend the dress rehearsal of every new show. This means, in reality there is no dress rehearsal, just two opening nights. Ridiculous! Everything had to be perfect for the planned dress rehearsal show.

In my first dress rehearsal, in a leading part on the professional stage, I understood a little of how Billy must have felt on that night at La Scala. There were two couples on stage with me. Suddenly I heard the prompter calling out a phrase and no one reacted. After four or

Monique with Egon Larsson, *Lock Up Your Daughters*, Stockholm, 1962

five calls from the prompter that could easily have been heard by the audience, I turned to Kjerstin Dellert and hissed the words, hoping she would pick up the cue. Then, as if struck by lightning, I realized it was my line! I wanted to disappear into a big black hole. The rest of the performance is a blur. Unbelievably not one newspaper critic picked up the unplanned silence.

Monique performing at Hamburger Bors in 1962

Chapter Seven

*If I weren't reasonably placid, I don't think
I could cope with this sort of life.
To be a diva, you've got to be absolutely like a horse.*
Dame Joan Sutherland

'Can't help loving that man of mine...'

*L*ock Up Your Daughters closed down after only two months and sixty performances.

This show opened for the first time at the Mermaid Theatre in London, in 1959. A production was planned to open on Broadway in 1960 but never got that far. In 1969 it was made into a film starring Christopher Plummer and Susannah York. Somehow English humour was lost on the Swedes.

The storyline is based on an eighteenth-century comedy, *Rape upon Rape*, by Henry Fielding and adapted by Bernard Miles. To me, it's really not much of a story-line, and the music isn't that interesting either.

During these two months I kept working on my voice and repertoire, preparing myself for more auditions. To do so I needed a new singing teacher situated in Stockholm and was told about a 'fabulous' teacher who, I was told, worked with some of the best singers.

I have now forgotten the name of this genius. All I can tell you is that I was more than excited when he told me on the phone that he had time to see me. Five minutes into the lesson he pointed to the waste-paper basket next to the piano, and told me it was there for me to spit in. I don't think I have spat more than ten times in my life. He must have seen the stunned expression on my face as he stood up and explained that if I wanted to sing I first had to get rid of all the mucus in my lungs. It was my belief that ladies do not spit, so the first lesson was also my last.

Next! Madame Skilondz, the big Russian prima donna who emigrated to Sweden during World War I. After she finished her career she began to teach singing in her grand apartment in Strandvagen, one of the most beautiful places in Stockholm.

The house was so majestic, I hardly dared to breathe as I walked up the stairs. A maid opened the front door and took me to the studio, where the diva, resplendent in full evening dress, was sitting like a statue on the piano chair. She did not move an inch or acknowledge my presence. I cleared my throat, preparing to introduce myself, when she waved her hand to indicate where she wanted me to stand.

I am a little annoyed that I cannot remember anything Madame Skilondz taught me. In the few times I saw her we did some scales and some old repertoire. I do not remember receiving any good advice or helpful comments.

I could not wait to get back to Gothenburg and start afresh with Alice. One of the most powerful techniques I learnt from Alice was to sing on the vowel 'ö'. It is magic. It helps project the voice forward whilst keeping everything open and free at the back of the mouth. I owe everything to this wonderful woman. Aside from good breath control and how to use my voice in a healthy way, she also taught me all about discipline and commitment.

Before I left Stockholm I had an audition for the part of Magnolia in *Show Boat*. Riksteatern was organizing a planned tour through the whole of Sweden commencing in August. Riksteatern was the largest touring theatre company in Sweden, and still is today. They don't just do musical productions but also opera, drama and ballet.

I always tell my students to be prepared for anything to happen especially at auditions. I also explain that if you can pull off good auditions, you are IN! The rest is easy. You will get all the help you need with the preparation for roles once you have been contracted. Occasionally you may be unlucky and find yourself working with people who are not so professional. You will then have to depend on your own experience to get you through. I am lucky that I have not had to do many auditions during my professional life but there is one audition imprinted on my memory.

Monique as Magnolia in *Show Boat*, Stockholm, 1963

Music and Love

I remember dressing up as well as I could for the audition for Magnolia in *Show Boat*. I had a new pair of very smart high-heeled shoes, and felt like a princess as I walked across the stage to begin my first song. Then one of my heels broke. I felt as if I had made an idiot of myself before I had even opened my mouth. I kicked the shoe into the wings, sang my songs and limped off.

I did get the part. I had shown that I could handle disasters on stage and continue on as though nothing had happened.

When *Show Boat* arrived on Broadway in 1927, it made an impact. The American music world was used to trivial and unrealistic operettas and light musical comedies. It brought a mixture of spectacle and seriousness – a complete new genre. Since there were no awards on Broadway in the 1920s, *Show Boat* had to wait until 1991 when it received the Laurence Olivier Award for Best Musical Revival. It also won the Tony Award for best Revival of a Musical in 1995.

The musical is based on Edna Ferber's best-selling novel of the same name. The story is about the lives of performers, stage-hands, and dock workers on *Cotton Blossom*, a Mississippi river boat, from 1887 to 1892. The music is by Jerome Kern and the book and lyrics are by Oscar Hammerstein .

Magnolia, the young daughter of the Captain on *Cotton Blossom*, was my first big role on the musical stage. To perform a part that covers forty years was a big task and taught me a lot. I would love to have performed the show in English, not Swedish and German. However, the English version of 'Can't help loving that man' has been part of my concert repertoire for years.

This was just the beginning of a long and very enjoyable relationship with Riksteatern. I stayed for another five years with them, building up my future repertoire of musicals, operettas and straight plays. I had leading roles in productions such as *Die Fledermaus, Orpheus in the Underworld* and *Dial M for Murder*.

Monique in *Orpheus and Eurydice* with Rutger Nygren, Stockholm, 1966

Monique with Rutger Nygren and Erna Skaug, 1966

Alfred Hitchcock produced and directed the film *Dial M for Murder* in 1954, with Grace Kelly and Ray Milland in the leading roles. The script was adapted from a successful stage play by Frederick Knott. In 2008 the film was chosen as the ninth best film in the mystery genre ever. The stage play on which the film was based was performed both in London and New York in 1952. The single setting in the stage play is the living room of Wendice's flat in London. Tony Wendice is planning to murder his wife, Margot, to inherit her life insurance. He has engaged a man to commit the crime in their apartment at a time when he himself is at work.

The cast of *Dial M for Murder*, Stockholm, 1967: seated, Lief Amble-Naess, Monique Brynnel; standing, left to right, Sten Gester, Roland Sandström, Ulf Lindquist

I was playing Margot during a live radio performance in Stockholm. As the murderer suddenly appeared in the apartment and tried to kill me, I grabbed a pair of scissors as rehearsed, I aimed for the hidden pocket in the back of his jacket. The scissors were supposed to appear as if they were driven straight into his ribs. Instead of him murdering Margot, he is murdered by Margot. Unfortunately I missed the pocket and the scissors fell on the floor and the public laughed. The whole plot was destroyed. The poor murderer had the presence of mind to act as if he was becoming unconscious and sort of dying from shock.

I have often wondered what on earth the radio listeners thought when they heard the audience laughing in that crucial dramatic scene.

Alice and Styrbjörn had a house in Asa on the West Coast, about an hour's drive from Gothenburg. This is where we spent most of our free time, especially during the summer. I had a wonderful holiday there spending lots of time on the beach, swimming and sailing. When I had time, after all the relaxing and having fun, I put my head in the score of *Show Boat*. I didn't feel I was under stress as the rehearsals were not due to start until the end of August.

Suddenly it *was* August, and I realized how silly I had been to leave it so late. I got a shock when I looked at the dialogue. My first line was, 'Do you live here? (Bor ni här?)' Four words. How simple, or so I thought until I discovered that those four words may be said in hundreds of different ways. Who was Magnolia? How did she feel when she was asking this? Why did she say it? How would the director want me to say it? What about the rest of the dialogue? I didn't get much sleep that night, or the next night. The day came when I had to face up to reality, the day that the rehearsals started in Stockholm. By then I had learnt my lesson and I promised myself that I would work hard and always be prepared in the future.

The ensemble met on 28 August and I can honestly say that we were a very happy group of people and got on extremely well. There was a good feeling from the beginning and all the rehearsals were most enjoyable. I was again the youngest and treated very kindly by everyone, even by the big names like Ingalill Söderman.

Show Boat, Stockholm, 1963, Monique as Magnolia, pictured with Rutger Nygren

Monique's Solo

When we were ready for the dress rehearsal, we moved to Avenyteatern in Ludvika, where the first night took place on 2 October. Everything went well, even my opening question 'Do you live here?' We had a happy eight months travelling and performing throughout Sweden.

Show Boat was a huge success. All the performers were, impressive and the production was remarkably entertaining. Some unforeseen things occurred, such as my half-wig falling off during a dance movement and my luggage disappearing for a couple of days. The bus also broke down many times during our travels. These were quite trivial events. Soon we, along with the rest of the world, were to be rocked by a dreadful tragedy.

On 22 November 1963 President Kennedy was assassinated in Dallas. A notice was posted on the main entrance of the hall to inform the patrons. We, the performers, were also told but didn't know that the audience was aware of what had happened. We decided not to tell them until the end of the show. When the leading man went out front after the last curtain call and announced the tragic event, we realized that the audience already knew. We were all numb from the horrendous news.

The Riksteatern company awards a scholarship every year to the most successful new artist and I was thrilled when it was presented to me in April 1964 at the end of the run of *Show Boat*. For the next four years, I spent eight months a year touring through the whole of Sweden. Touring is an art in itself. The first thing to do in the morning is check that physically you are healthy with no sign of a cold or flu. As there was no understudy, this became important. Luckily, I never had to cancel a performance.

Then it's time to get organized, pack your things, have breakfast with the rest of the cast who are at the same hotel as you, then off to the bus. After ten minutes in the bus most of us were asleep and unaware of the landscape we were passing through. After unloading the luggage at the hotel at the next city, there would be time for a quick lunch and then another couple of hours of sleep. I often felt that all I did was sleep. About 6.00 pm I went to the theatre to check out the acoustics and the backstage facilities, and prepare for the performance. After the performance, dinner was the highlight of the day. It was possible to relax and indulge in some delicious food at the hotel. It was a time to discuss the performance and have a few laughs.

Monique in *Die keusche Susanne*, Stockholm, 1966

Chapter Eight

Those who wish to sing, always find a song.
Swedish proverb

'I can't give you anything but love...'

In the middle of my summer holidays, I had a call from the Culture Ministry in Stockholm, asking if I was free and would I be interested in going to Russia for a one month's concert tour. As this happened to be when the Wall was still up in Berlin and Khruschev was the man in charge, I hesitated. But only for a second so I could take a deep breath and scream, 'Yes of course!'

It was the first time Sweden had sent a single artist to Russia. I wonder if others were a little wiser and wary of travelling solo behind the Iron Curtain. For those born after the Wall fell, it will be difficult to understand the political tension between Eastern and Western Europe between 1945 and 1989. People living close to the border lived in constant fear that another war would break out.

I entered a huge, totally empty Russian plane in Copenhagen in July 1964. Eight stewardesses looked after me. When we passed over Estonia, the captain's voice cut through the air. 'We are now leaving the western world'. That's when it hit me. What on earth was I doing? Why hadn't anybody stopped me? I felt very uneasy.

One of the stewardesses passed on a request from the captain to come to the pilot's cabin. I sat between the captain and the co-pilot for the rest of the journey. I am sure they thought they were giving me a treat, but I am terrified of flying and never look out the plane window.

Worse was to come. Getting off the plane in Moscow, I was met by hundreds of people. Some were from the Russian Culture Ministry, and some were from the media. Some were probably there because they didn't believe that someone would choose to come, leaving the free world. The whole orchestra was there. After having been welcomed by a group of politicians, I saw a woman being pushed towards me.

'Welcome to Moscow', she said in perfect Oxford English.

'My name is Helga Laane', she added. 'I will be your interpreter and dresser during your visit.'

Helga became much more than that. She became one of my closest friends until her death some thirty years later.

Helga explained to me that the conductor of the orchestra would like to have the sheet music of the songs I was going to perform. I handed them the three Swedish songs suggested by the people from the Swedish Culture Ministry, believing that was all I was expected to do. There was silence before I was informed that they expected me to perform solo for at least forty-five minutes. I was aghast.

There was some discussion before Helga translated the conductor's request. 'Our conductor is wondering if it would be all right to add some standard jazz songs into your program.'

I was amazed. Could this really be true? I was in Russia and they were asking me to perform American music. People were being jailed for listening to this type of music. All I could do was agree.

Helga and I were escorted to another plane to St. Petersburg. This was a totally different experience to the plane from Copenhagen. For a start, next to me was a man who had a goat on his knee! During the flight I was aware that Helga didn't say much and the reason became clear later.

Boris, a representative from the Culture Ministry, met us at the airport and drove us to the Hotel Europa. It was not very grand but it would do. I was happy to get to the hotel to have an early night. I noticed that there was a 'watchdog' sitting at a desk on every floor. What I didn't notice was the tape recorder stuck to the ceiling in my bedroom. It was a shock when I walked into my hotel room one day, and found two men changing tapes!

I didn't know what to expect at the rehearsals the following day, and felt a bit apprehensive. I need not have worried. The orchestra members were so kind, and very excited. This was not so much about me but more about having the opportunity to play jazz! They were all living dangerously, listening not only to outlawed music but also to news from the United States. The only opportunity to perform jazz was when accompanying a foreign guest artist who would sing that genre. So I was very popular.

The first concert took place the following day. I managed to learn a Russian folk-song and proudly performed it. I had written one verse on my left hand and one on my right in case I forgot a word. This was a great success and the audience loved the jazz.

After the concert, Boris invited Helga and me to share caviar and champagne at a lovely restaurant. They clearly wanted to share some thoughts with me and so we agreed to meet the next day for a walk in the park. This was one of the few places to talk without being recorded. We met the next day and I listened while they talked.

Helga was from Estonia. Her husband owned a big shipping business in Tallinn. Her life changed the day the Russians came to Tallinn during the war. She did not know what happened to her husband, but Helga herself was sent to Moscow after it was discovered that she spoke five languages. She became a full-time interpreter. After the war, she ended up in St Petersburg and she had been living in the same place for almost twenty years. Her home was a part of room that was divided by curtains into four spaces, and shared by another three families. Helga arrived at the hotel one day, crying with happiness because she had been given a new place to live. It was a garage! For her it was heaven after sharing a room with three families for a long time. She could now close the door and have her privacy. She was told she could return to Estonia at the age of seventy-five. I know the thought of being back where she belonged kept her going. That special day came, about twenty-three years later.

Boris was a public figure, so I was careful never to go into details about his conversation with me when I returned to Sweden. He told me that he would do anything to be able to escape to the West. He wasn't married and had no family, so escaping to the West would not involve heartbreak or retaliation for any relatives.

Jazz concert in Leningrad, 1964

The concerts had a good run and the huge response, especially to the American repertoire, amazed me.

One night there was an incident that has lived in my memory ever since. I had just finished a song and during the applause I noticed an old lady dressed in black with a scarf over her head walking up the middle aisle. She stopped in front of the stage and handed me a piece of wet and torn fabric. I opened it and found three half dead wildflowers inside. It took time for me to recover from the emotion that swept over me. I wanted to hold her in my arms.

We took the concert to Kronstadt, an island that belonged to Finland until the war. Russia used it as a military base. We travelled there by private ship.

I wanted to unburden myself of some luggage so I asked Helga to take me to the concert hall. She continued walking towards a church and I realized that this was where the concert was to be held. We opened the side door and were hit by total darkness. When my eyes adjusted I realized that the church was full of soldiers. I turned my head in the direction of the altar and there, instead of the altar, was a screen showing a violent war film!

I got rid of my bags and left. Helga and I found an eatery with one dish on the menu. I had been taught not to ask about meat. If it wasn't mentioned on a menu then there was no meat. In 1964, there were only six or seven towns in Russia that had restaurants offering meat. I got my food, but they forgot to bring me a knife or so I thought. Helga knew better: 'If you're not brought something specific, that means they haven't got it. So – just eat and be quiet.'

It felt strange to be standing in this unknown church belting out some 'naughty' jazz songs like 'I can't give you anything but love....' for a horde of Russian soldiers.

After the concert I went for a walk by myself to the harbour, while the musicians and Helga packed the instruments. It would have been sensible to wait for the musicians but I wanted some fresh air. It was pitch dark when I arrived at the harbour. The ship that had brought us to Kronstadt was tied up, waiting to take us back to St Petersburg. There were no lights on the wharf or the ship itself so my next move was more than stupid.

I attempted to jump onto the ship, but landed in the water between the ship and the wharf. It took some time before people heard my screams and came to find out what was happening. They tried to find me in the black water. It seemed like an eternity before

I was pulled up on deck. I still have a scar on my right leg to remind me of that night. I thought I was going to die and wondered what my family's reaction would be to being told I had disappeared in the sea after a concert at Kronstadt. Because of the political climate at the time they might find it difficult to believe it was a simple accident.

I had the pleasure of being invited as a guest on a couple of televison talk shows in St Petersburg, where I sang my jazz repertoire. Several years later I had a letter from Helga telling me that they were repeating my appearances on television over and over.

One day Boris took me aside and told me not to be worried.

'About what?' I asked. It turned out that the Americans had identified a Russian ship near the coast of Cuba. The Russians said it was full of people holidaying. 'Nothing will happen' he said. 'Right now Russia can only maintain a war economically for one and a half days. Anyway, every intelligent Russian who hears or reads about this knows that we haven't got any people who can afford to go on a cruise like that. You'll soon be safely back in Sweden.'

I was really beginning to worry and began to count the days before I could leave.

I left Russia on 27 August, promising Goskonzerts and friends I would definitely be back soon. To my embarrassment I have never set foot in Russia again. After the third new invitation, I received an official statement to the effect that they would not invite me again. It was obvious that I was not interested in more engagements in Russia.

Chapter Nine

Where words leave off, music begins.
Heinrich Heine

Boeing Boeing...and touring Europe

After my trip to Russia, I was very happy to become involved with *Boeing Boeing* which was being staged at Lisebergsteatern in Gothenburg. This was to be my second straight acting part and once again I became aware of how much easier it is to perform as an actor compared to a singer.

Whether a singer or an actor, preparation is essential. Imagine this evening you are to perform Desdemona in Verdi's *Othello*. If you wake up with a sore throat, there is a big risk that you will have to cancel tonight's performance. If you do go on stage you are under enormous pressure, fearful that your performance will not be up to your normal standards. Your timing must be perfect from beginning to end as there is a person with a baton standing in the pit controlling every single sound coming out of your mouth. Half a second too early or too late and you have failed.

A singer must have absolute control of when and where to breathe. Imagine, in the middle of an aria, getting a tickle in your throat or too much saliva in your mouth and an urge to swallow. You cannot stop and get rid of it. The music keeps going.

You may have sung perfectly for two hours and on the last note in your last aria, your voice cracks. That crack is what the audience will remember and talk about on their way home. The fact that your performance until then was superb is totally unimportant.

On the other hand, imagine you are performing the role of Desdemona in Shakespeare's *Othello*.

If you wake up with a sore throat it is not such a problem. You don't even have to bother about warming up your voice. You might be a bit hoarse, have to clear your voice, breathe in different places than usual, or talk a bit faster. This is a nuisance but you are not chained to a score or a person with a baton. You don't have to worry about anyone noticing if you happen to take a longer pause at a certain place, because of phlegm. It's all about how convincing you are in portraying Desdemona.

For me, there is nothing as exciting as a performer with a sublime voice who is also a convincing actor.

To be a singer on stage is really hard work and being a male singer can be even harder. I'm told tenors are advised not to perform any physical exercise for one or two days prior to a performance. As it is a normal occurrence to have two or three performances a week, wives can become quite frustrated, and I should know!

Boeing Boeing was the most performed French play throughout the world in 1991. It was written by Marc Camoletti and staged for the first time in London in 1962, and ran for a total of seven years. It is a light comedy about three stewardesses, French, German and English and how they manage to fit their love lives into their changeable daily timetable.

Ironically, I do not enjoy flying and have never understood how anyone can choose to have a profession which involves spending time in the air.

I played the part of the Lufthansa stewardess, Martha. On the first night, I nearly fell off my dressing-room chair when a stage-hand came to inform me that the performance had started. I was used to hearing the orchestra tuning up before every performance. It was a most eerie feeling stepping out on stage in total silence.

Boeing Boeing, Gothenburg, 1964: from left, standing: Karl-Arne Holmsten, Berndt Westerberg, Egon Larsson; seated Monique, Mona Åstrand and Solweig Lagström

On the last night I was invited to a party after the show. My role as Martha called for me to wear a very sexy nightgown in the final scene. In the break between my last appearance and the curtain call I had quickly changed into my warm and cosy woollen underwear so I would be ready to run off to the party. Not very pretty, but nobody would see that because I put the sexy nightgown back on over the top. I made my entrance running in through a side door. My sexy nightgown got caught in the door handle and Miss Martha was seen by everybody in her daggy granny underwear.

It was a splendid finale and farewell to *Boeing Boeing* and to a most enjoyable period playing Martha.

My next engagement was to perform as Rosalinda in *Die Fledermaus* at the Riksteatern in Stockholm. Rosalinda was then, and is still, one of my favourite roles. I felt Rosalinda fitted me like a glove. The tessitura is just right for my voice and so is the character. Ironically, I was to have more success later when singing Adele, the other female lead.

Die Fledermaus was staged for the first time in the Theater an der Wien in 1874, and has been in the repertoire of this theatre ever since. Johann Strauss, the composer, conducted the first performance in Vienna. It was an immediate success and is still one of the most performed operettas in the world.

The comedy revolves around Rosalinda, the wife of a flirtatious husband, Gabriel. She disguises herself and appears at a party where her husband is having a good time. Gabriel becomes interested in this good-looking and interesting woman in a mask. Unaware that she is his own wife, he starts flirting with her.

Die Fledermaus, with Carrie Nielson, Stockholm, 1965

The music is wonderful and definitely one of my favourite operettas. I have had the pleasure of performing this operetta in Swedish, German and English in Stockholm, Munich and Sydney.

The rehearsals and performances were very rewarding and I believe everybody involved enjoyed being part of this production just as much as I did.

I was able to fit in a couple of auditions in Germany between the different productions with Riksteatern. One audition was for the lead in *The Merry Widow* at Gartnerplatztheater in Munich. My first audition managed to gain the attention of the intendant, Dr Pscherer, and the next audition in full costume was to take place a couple of weeks later. I remember walking around the theatre in the costume of the Widow for half an hour waiting for Dr Pscherer to arrive. I had a wonderful feeling that I was already part of the institution.

I got the contract and ended up staying in that production for eight years. *The Merry Widow* was planned to start at the beginning of 1969 and to our great excitement was scheduled as one of the main performances during the Olympics in 1972. Not everything works out as planned, even when contracted. It turned out the renovations of the Opera House that were due to be finished in the summer of 1968 required another fifteen months. *The Merry Widow* was postponed for a year.

Chapter Ten

When you hear music you are not alone.
Robert Browning

'I've found your Danilo!'

My first engagement on the Continent was the leading part in *The Gypsy Princess* in the Sommerfestspiele at the Stadtstheater, Baden bei Wien. Being aware that I might get into some difficulties having never been in a German production before, I made sure I knew my part backwards. I could not have had a nicer introduction to the German 'music world'. Everything fell into place. Even though I was aware of my Swedish accent, I got the feeling that people actually enjoyed it. It probably gave them something to laugh at. I was again lucky to have wonderful, professional people to work with and again to make friends for life. The production ran for two months during the summer of 1968 and during our free days, friends and colleagues introduced me to wonderful Vienna.

One place I regret visiting was a natural hot sulphur spa, where I picked up a virus that caused me to develop tinnitus in my ears. I honestly thought I was going crazy on that first night when I noticed the ringing in my ear. The noise kept me awake and I became increasingly worried about what was going to happen on stage, if the sound didn't disappear. I was a wreck in the morning. I arranged appointments with two different doctors. Both said they could not do anything except advise me not to worry, even though I was stuck with this noise for the rest of my life. As far as they knew it would not interfere with my hearing or have any other side effects.

The Gypsy Princess, Baden bei Wien, 1968, with Josef Ebner (left) and Heinz Zednik

That was almost fifty years ago. My tinnitus is still there and growing strongly in both ears. At the moment I am being entertained by five different sounds twenty-four hours a day. I would love to be able to record this sound phenomenon and perhaps put it on You Tube. On a serious note, I have been able to help other people with tinnitus through talking realistically and positively about the problem. It is not painful, you will survive, you need to accept it and try to be as strong as you can psychologically. Otherwise it can have devastating effects on your life.

The director of *The Gypsy Princess* wanted the leading man to pick me up and carry me off the stage after one duet. At the dress rehearsal the tenor picked me up and carried me into the wings. Then he fainted. I would like to say it was the excitement of carrying me but unfortunately it turned out to be a heart problem. Luckily we had a doctor in the house, who examined the tenor and pronounced him well enough to continue. There was no further talk of carrying me off.

I was invited to be a guest in a radio talk show in Vienna and asked if I would sing a short song on the program. There was a brilliant pianist there and a beautiful grand piano so I didn't mind at all. I didn't have any sheet music with me so I decided to choose something I thought everyone would know. The film *Sound of Music* had just become a huge success around the world so I suggested 'Edelweiss'.

The producer and the pianist looked at each other with a blank face and then turned to me. 'Did you say Edelweiss? Where is that from?' I thought they were joking, but it became clear that they really didn't know the song or the show so I selected something else. A friend told me later that in 1968 *Sound of Music* was prohibited from being shown and broadcast in Austria.

My manager sent me to audition in Kiel, where they planned a *Merry Widow* to start in January 1969. That engagement would then fill in the space before I started in Munich, and I would also gain good experience in the role.

Alice, Styrbjörn and I had planned a holiday driving down to Italy so it suited us perfectly to stop over in Kiel. *Lohengrin* happened to be playing at the opera house on the day we arrived, and Alice and Styrbjörn decided to go to the performance. I was told to rest and prepare myself for the audition the following day.

I was awake when they came home. Alice was beside herself with excitement as she told me she had found my Danilo, the male lead in *The Merry Widow*. Obviously Mr Lohengrin himself had sung himself into her heart. Styrbjörn seemed to be very impressed as well. I found it difficult to imagine that a Wagnerian tenor would be suited to the role of Danilo.

I did the audition next morning and was offered the part. The artistic director warned me that they didn't have a Danilo yet. Their tenor had refused to do it. He had sung Danilo more than any other tenor in the world and he was not interested in doing operetta any more. He was of course the Lohengrin who had so impressed Alice. A couple of months later, I found myself sharing a compartment in a train to Munich with a very nice gentleman. He happened to be a baritone and was working in Kiel. We started chatting and I told him about *The Merry Widow* problem, whereupon he laughed. The tenor who played Lohengrin and had turned down the part of Danilo was his best friend and he was fully aware of the situation.

I am flattered to think he must have thought I wasn't too bad, because he mentioned to his tenor friend that he had met the Widow on the train. Whatever he said made the tenor change his mind and accept the role. This was to have an impact on both the tenor's and my own life.

Duet

Chapter One

*These two are not two, love has made them one. Amo Ergo Sum!
And by its mystery each is no less but more.*
Benjamin Britten

Kiel, 1969: the man with the voice

The conductor of *The Merry Widow*, Karl Eckert, greeted me when I stepped off the ferry from Gothenburg. It was 9.00 am and we went straight to the Opera House situated on a beautiful lake in the middle of Kiel. The original building was destroyed during the war and was not rebuilt until fifteen years later.

After breakfast, we went to room 320 to run through the music. I was relieved that it was just me and Karl to begin with. The tenor was due to arrive an hour later.

One hour later, Jon Weaving, my husband to be, walked in. I have thought about this moment a lot, and I'm not sure if it was love at first sight. I think I was too nervous for my hormones to activate, even though there was a stunning man standing next to me singing his heart out. I listened to the voice and something stirred in my mind. I knew I had heard that voice before, but couldn't recall exactly where and when. It all fell into place during the break a couple of hours later.

While enjoying a cup of coffee together, it was as though I was suddenly hit by lightning! Was it the coffee, the surroundings or the man himself? We both found it incredible that our voices had already met through the Wigmore Hall's studio walls some seven years earlier. Somehow we felt we were not strangers but that we already, in a way impossible to describe, belonged together. The two people who went back to the rehearsal were not the same people who had left thirty minutes earlier. We were a pair!

And now I could simply write 'and the next is history'. And it is! But it is so rich, that I want to share it with you.

The opera house had organized an apartment for me in a private house that was owned by a lovely couple, the Vollandts. I stayed with them until both Jon and I felt we just had to live together. The turning point came one morning when I woke up and found a note under the door from Jon, saying he had been missing me. Despite throwing snowballs at my window (I lived on the second floor) he was unable to wake me. So I moved to Jon's place which also was closer to town and the opera house.

It was now I acquired another name, created by Jon: 'Pferd', which means 'horse' in English. He told me he happened to be looking out the window from his dressing room when he saw me walking away. My hair was hanging like a horse's tail down my back, hence the name. This time I loved my new name and still do.

The rehearsals went well and were enthralling. The time came closer and closer for the final rehearsal where we were expected to show our full potential. So we had our first kiss in public on stage!

Lehár's music is very beautiful but strangely, even though it sounds as if it's easy to sing, it is definitely not! I have now performed in hundreds of performances in different productions of *The Merry Widow* and have never been able to relax. I have always found the character of Hanna Glawari a bit impersonal. Having said that, I enjoyed the Kiel production more than anything I had been involved with up till then. Is there anything as indescribably wonderful as being in love? I don't think so!

Jon and Monique, *The Merry Widow*, Kiel, 1969

I had found a wonderful singing coach, Annie Rohling, in Kiel. I also introduced Jon to her and he was very impressed. He had been looking for a long time in Germany for someone who could coach him with his Wagnerian repertoire. Annie was perfect. She had been a leading Wagnerian soprano in Berlin before the war and had a wonderful knowledge and technique to share. Her technique was simple and straight to the point. Her teachings did not clash with anything he already knew and had been using and that was the cream on the cake. He was immediately impressed as Annie's technique was based on singing 'schlank' not 'spread'. 'Schlank' describes a method where the shape of the mouth is narrowed, dropping the jaw and enabling the throat to become open and frees the true voice to emerge. 'Spread' creates more tension in the voice and alters the sound, making it more nasal and tight. It is a self-made sound using muscles inside and has nothing to do with voice production.

I remember becoming quite emotional when Annie told us about the suffering after the war. She pulled a cart carrying her mother, trying to escape the Russians. We all became very close and, we kept in contact with Annie until she passed away some twenty years later.

Another wonderful woman to whom I was extremely close was Gertie, my dresser. Our first meeting was a bit of a shock for Gertie. It was the day of the first dress rehearsal. I was sitting in front of the mirror making myself ready for the performance, and I could see Gertie organizing my costumes behind me. Something went wrong with my hair and my reaction was a simple 'Scheisse!' In the mirror, I could see Gertie stop what she was doing and she called out curtly, 'A lady doesn't use such words!' I was taught a lesson. This word sounds like 'shit' in Oxford English but is in fact a word we Swedes are brought up with and use as almost a 'sweet' comment.

In spite of what Gertie thought was my unladylike behavior, she accepted having me around and thank goodness she did. She remained my dresser for another four productions. To illustrate how close we got, Gertie was the first person to know when I became pregnant, after Jon, of course.

Gertie, my friend and dresser

Alice and Styrbjörn came down to Kiel for the premier on 29 January, and they were very impressed. I kept my little secret to myself for the time being, but I'm sure they could feel there was more than a professional connection between this Danilo and Hanna Glawari.

The first kiss in public, in *The Merry Widow*, Kiel, 1969

The newspaper critics perhaps also felt the difference as *The Merry Widow* became a huge success and Jon and I became the perfect leading couple. The public could somehow connect with us. Jon was at that time the tenor who had sung more performances as Danilo than any other singer in the world. He was not aware of this until he visited the Lehár Museum in Salzburg, and read the statement under a picture of himself. I, on the other hand, performing Hanna Glawari for the first time in my life, found the experience both scary and interesting.

Jon was singing lead roles, not just in operas like *Hoffman's Erzahlungen* and *Othello* during this season in Kiel but also in the Wagnerian repertoire like *Lohengrin*. His portrayal of Lohengrin was mesmerizing and I totally understood Alice's excitement when she saw his performance six months earlier.

Jon started off his professional career as a baritone and it was not until he embarked on the German stage that he was ready to change 'Fach'. This he did to great success. He had everything, an impressive stage presence and a unique and unusual timbre to his voice. On top of that, I don't think I have ever met anyone with such knowledge and love for music, and especially the human voice.

There was also something else that could make one believe in reincarnation. Later, in Australia, I met Molly, who was one of the best pianists I have ever met. Molly used to accompany Jon when he was only about twelve years old. She told me it didn't matter what music she gave him – old Italian arias or German Lieder, he would take one look at it and, without getting any information or advice, would sing the music as the composer had wanted it to be. How can one explain this?

Life was wonderful, and continued, if possible, to get even better. One night during the performance of the merry widow waltz, I whispered to Jon, 'Let's get married!'

He had the chance to disagree, or did he? I had my heel on his toe.

Jon in *Othello*, Kiel, 1969

We became engaged on my birthday, 28 April and celebrated at home where Jon prepared the most wonderful dinner. He was a fantastic cook and loved every minute in the kitchen. Next to cooking, ironing was Jon's big passion. As I loathe cooking as much as ironing, we were a perfect pair.

Music and Love

Our engagement celebration dinner, cooked by Jon,
28 April 1969

After we became engaged, it was time to let Alice and Styrbjörn know that I had a man in my life. No comment in the world would have made me change the situation. To my surprise, they were ecstatic and wanted us to come up and stay with them for a couple of days. As soon as we had some free days we drove up to Asa, their summer place. We had a couple of really relaxing and happy days, except that Alice would not let us share a bedroom, since we were not married. We decided to speed up the wedding date.

Chapter Two

What force is more potent than love?
Igor Stravinsky

The wedding

Jon was engaged to sing the part of Bacchus in the English National Opera's production of *Ariadne auf Naxos* at the Coliseum in London from June to August in 1969. We departed for England as soon as the season finished in Kiel and found a lovely apartment in Westminster Mansions, next to Westminster Abbey in the middle of London.

I have never been to as many wonderful performances in such a short time. This was a very different visit to London to my last one when I was there on my scholarship seven years previously. While Jon worked, I was free to go to the theatre.

One memorable experience was seeing Sir John Gielgud in a performance at the National Theatre of Great Britain. A friend who worked in the ensemble told us that during a rehearsal Sir John noticed a stage-hand who happened to be standing absolutely still behind him. He calmly announced to the stage-hand, 'No one but me, is allowed to do nothing on stage!'

He understood how to get an audience's attention, and that is performing wisdom.

As a Viking woman, I proposed to my husband and put my foot down about what sort of wedding it was to be. A five-minute ceremony at Caxton Hall sounded perfect to me – no long ceremony, no guest list of hundreds, no coach and none of the circus elements.

I told my mother that Jon and I were to be married. Two weeks later I received a letter in response, which began – 'Dear Monica! WHY?' It was some time before I realized why she had sent this. To her, I was living the life she had enjoyed before she married. I had a career and I shared the stage with the man I loved. This would have been her dream. To her, marriage meant having children and becoming a housewife. She did not understand that today a woman can chose to have a profession, a family or both.

Things did not run smoothly. We were unable to make a booking for the wedding, because we were waiting for some official papers to arrive from Germany. On the second-last day of our stay in London we still had not received them. On the last day, late in the morning, the papers finally arrived and we immediately rang Caxton Hall. Luckily someone had cancelled and we managed to arrange an appointment for 3.00 pm. There was just enough time to clean the apartment, pack our luggage and get ready for the big event. We were intending to drive to Dover after Jon's performance on that evening. We planned to catch a ferry to France and then drive for ten hours to Kiel, where rehearsals started the next day.

While I was trying on clothes, deciding what to wear, Jon rushed out and found me a bouquet of yellow roses.

We had not thought about witnesses for the wedding. Jon should have had a peaceful afternoon preparing himself for his performance. Instead he had some stressful hours ahead, trying to find two friends who would not mind being our witnesses despite the short notice. I was no help as I didn't know many people in London. Luckily Jon found two friends who were happy to meet us at the appointed time at Caxton Hall.

We arrived there at about 2.50 pm to find Jon's friends there. After five minutes' waiting, my stomach began to bother me and, feeling nauseated, I retired to the toilet. Jon began to knock on the door and I remember shaking and hanging on to my little teddy bear that I had brought along as a good luck mascot. I dragged myself out of the toilet to find a slightly annoyed groom standing outside the door. We were pushed into a room where two officials were standing with the two witnesses. One of the officials read something I didn't understand and then asked if I, Monica Margareta Brynnel agreed. I realized that the answer had to be 'Yes'.

The wedding day

Mrs Monica Weaving left Caxton Hall with her husband and the two witnesses. We headed for the pub across the road, where we had a quick cup of coffee and a slice of cheesecake. See how easy it can be!

I spent the evening at the Coliseum, one of the largest opera houses, enjoying *Ariadne auf Naxos* together with Dr Alfred Alexander, who looked after Jon's vocal cords and also the precious throats of the Royal Family. Alfred had insisted on inviting us for a wedding breakfast after Jon's performance. The three of us had a lovely time although Jon and I had to be careful not to consume the champagne that was offered. After midnight we left for Dover where we caught the ferry. I'm sure there are better ways to spend a wedding night…

The day after our romantic wedding, Jon and I arrived in Kiel, quite exhausted, but still very happy. Jon had a lazy, spoilt cat called Rick who made a small effort to show some excitement about our return.

Life returned to normal with rehearsals and coaching with Annie. Buying a double bed made us feel really married.

One week later Jon had to fly back to London for more performances of *Ariadne*. This was sad and the first of many separations to come. Our lives as performers meant we were frequently apart because of engagements in different places.

The season in Kiel began with *Fidelio* and Florestan became one of Jon's favourite roles. It may have been because Florestan doesn't appear until the second act and the role calls for him to look dirty and unshaven, so not much preparation was required. However, Florestan's main aria is like an Olympic high jump. The tessitura keeps going higher and higher and even higher towards the end. I'm glad I'm not a dramatic tenor.

Jon had a very busy season with *Faust* by Gounod coming up next.

I absolutely adored Jon in this production. It suited him as a person and the 'fach' was not as demanding. His singing could be more relaxed. 'Fach' refers to the style of singing. For example the style can be Italian, Wagnerian, romantic or lyrical.

The first performance as a married couple in *The Merry Widow* during the new season was very special. The newspapers had reported our wedding and we received a standing ovation at the end of the first act. I still have some of the heart-warming written messages we received from people in the audience.

Jon in *Faust*, Kiel, 1969

We had a couple of days free and drove to Sweden. (This time we were allowed to share a bedroom at Alice and Styrbjörn's house.)

My mother Greta and my sister Rosa invited us to a restaurant where they were serving something best translated as a 'black soup'. This was a culinary first for Jon. In Sweden, there are numerous official celebrations through the year. At this time Sweden was celebrating 'Marten Gas' or Marten the Goose, hence the black soup (blood soup). The taste is not too bad but it is difficult to disregard what you are actually putting in your mouth.

Jon kept a straight face and swallowed the dark liquid but I think he was happy to get back to a more civilized cuisine.

Chapter Three

*Music is the divine way to tell beautiful,
poetic things to the heart.*
Pablo Casals

The Merry Widow, Munich, 1970–78

November arrived and it was time for me to start rehearsals for *The Merry Widow* in Munich.

The Merry Widow, an operetta in three acts by Franz Lehár, was an overwhelming success on its first performance and gave Lehár international recognition as a composer. It has continued to delight audiences ever since. Set in Paris, the love story revolves around Prince Danilo and the merry widow, Hanna Glawari. The waltz 'Lippen schweigern' is beautiful and one of the most well-known love duets in operetta.

This was something I had been looking forward to with great excitement before I met Jon. The excitement turned to sorrow as the day got closer when I had to leave. Jon promised to come to Munich a week later and this eased the pain of parting a little.

I am not sure how old the Gartnerplatztheater is, but there is a glorious theatrical atmosphere in the auditorium itself. Forty years ago, backstage was not so great. There were only a couple of dressing rooms for the soloists, so I shared a room with three other female singers. It was actually lots of fun and I got to know my colleagues better and more quickly than if I had been by myself. Being newly married and missing my husband desperately made me the butt of jokes from my new female friends. They talked to me like old, wise nannies and predicted that it would not be long before I would be blessing the days that I didn't have to see the man I was married to.

The rehearsals were a bit tough as everybody was trying to be as good as they could possibly be. Most of the ensemble were guests and met for the first time in rehearsal. My Danilo was a man from Vienna who was nothing in comparison to my Jon, but of course I am completely biased.

Kurt Pscherer, the chief of the opera house and director of *The Merry Widow*, had a very strong personality, and people were scared of him. He only had to wave one of his little fingers and everyone, especially in the female ensemble, would obey him. Except me.

The two final weeks before the premiere on 16 January went extremely fast. Jon arrived for the last dress rehearsal and was able to give me important feedback. His main comments were about how horrendous the last curtain call was. Pscherer had decided to show a huge picture of starving African children above the heads of the cast while we were taking the final applause. We, the cast, were unaware that this was happening.

I'm not sure if his plan was to create a scandal for the purpose of getting as much publicity as possible. (It doesn't matter what the papers write as long as they write something.) Creating scandal around a production seems to have become a tradition over the last twenty years, particularly in Germany. It seems to work, inasmuch that people who had not planned to go to a new show turn up, if only to check if it is really as bad as the papers say.

The premiere was a big success until the last curtain call. The audience booed Pscherer off the stage. Everyone was shocked by the sudden appearance of the picture swinging above the heads of the cast. But Pscherer's plan worked. The critics were appalled and tore his idea to pieces. Luckily everything else received only praise. After the premiere the picture of the starving children was never seen again and *The Merry Widow* stayed in the repertoire in the Opera House at Gartnerplatz for over eight years. And so did I.

To celebrate my first night in Munich, Jon and I shared a little bit too much champagne. It did not affect Jon adversely but I woke up with my first and last hangover. I had to beg Jon to find a chemist and find something that could get me going. I had a matinee at

The Merry Widow, Munich, 1970

Music and Love

The Merry Widow, Munich, 1971

1.00 pm. I felt absolutely terrible and very nervous about the performance. Somehow I got through and believe me, there was no more champagne for a very long time!

Pscherer offered me a new two-year guest contract a couple of weeks later, which I gladly signed.

The next premiere in the Weaving family was *Rheingold* in Kiel, the first opera in Wagner's *Ring* cycle, where Jon sang Loge. I had a performance in Munich the night before and the night after and told Jon that I would miss the premiere as I had to stay in Munich. He believed me.

I arrived just in time for the performance and had managed to get a seat on the side of the first balcony, five metres from the stage.

Jon was delivering a great performance both acting and musically, when in the middle of a phrase, his eyes wandered up towards where I was sitting. I don't think anyone but the conductor would have been aware of the sudden short pause in Jon's singing. Jon was thrilled and surprised that I had managed to get there, although I think perhaps Wagner would have protested loudly.

Kiel Opera House put on a production of *Can Can* for me. The rehearsals were to start in mid-March. This suited me very well as I only had one or two performances a week at that time in Munich.

Can Can is a delightful Cole Porter musical comedy set in Paris at the turn of the century. The story concerns the showgirls of the Montmartre dance halls during the 1890s. It ran for over two years on Broadway.

At the dress rehearsal we found that I was one costume short. Nothing suitable was found in the old costume department. It was Saturday morning and there was no fabric and no design. This particular costume was supposed to be the highlight of the night. The costume people rushed into town and found some black sequinned material, which they transformed into a straight slim-line long dress. Wow! It became the costume of the night and I still have it. It was just so perfect that I bought it from the opera house when *Can Can* finished and have worn it more than any other dress I have ever had.

At this stage Jon was appearing in *Pagliacci,* an opera by Ruggero Leoncavallo about a clown thwarted in love who murders the object of his affection. The audience was surprised when Jon's first entrance was on a real motor-bike! Being a clown himself, he had fun musically and in putting on a clown face.

The Can Can dress

Chapter Four

*To sing opera, one needs two things:
the voice and the passion – and above all, the passion.*
Andrea Bocelli

The honeymoon…eventually

One year after our wedding, we at last had enough free time to have a brief honeymoon. It was wonderful and worth waiting for.

We departed Munich after the last performance of *The Merry Widow* for the season. We drove to Seefeld then from Austria through to Switzerland and then to La Trayas on the French Riviera, and stayed in a great hotel overlooking the water.

I love the Mediterranean. We had brought with us a rubber boat, hardly big enough for a baby, but big enough for us to have lots of fun in the water.

We then spent some time in Portofino. In the 1970s it was easier to walk around peacefully than it is today. We moved on to Verona where we experienced a wonderful performance of *Carmen* with my second favourite tenor, Franco Corelli. We were told that a horse had fallen off the stage into the orchestra pit during a performance a couple of nights earlier. No one was hurt but no doubt the horse was not very happy.

Music and Love

Then to Venice, which became one of our favourite places. We sat by the Ponte de Rialto enjoying a couple of glasses of champagne and admiring the gondolas and boats passing by. We saw a group of people in one of the bus boats waving insanely towards where we were sitting. We took no notice, thinking it was nothing to do with us. A couple of weeks later, some of the singers in the chorus in Kiel accused us of being rude then we realized that they were the ones waving, and they were waving to us!

Belated honeymoon in Austria, 1970

We moved on to Pula, in former Yugoslavia, where we planned to stay for a week. The weather was lovely, the beach beautiful, the hotel pleasant, but the food was dreadful. Even I felt desperate for some real food after a couple of days. We lasted five days then decided this was enough and headed for home.

Two days later, we were back in Kiel. Rick, our cat, was not impressed. The next day Jon and I looked at each other. What were we doing? We had two more weeks of holidays left. Were we mad? Why did we leave the Mediterranean? We rushed off to the travel bureau and bought tickets for a flight. Next day we were back in Yugoslavia. This time we had a week of sun, water and good food. We were also able to squeeze in one week of holidays in Sweden before the rehearsals.

The new season commenced in September, 1970. The opera house in Kiel staged a new production of *The Count of Luxembourg* with Jon and myself as the romantic leads. This is an operetta in two acts with English lyrics and music by Franz Lehár. Dr Klaiber, the director of the opera, didn't bother to ask Jon this time if he wanted to do another operetta. Jon was also rehearsing *Boris Gudonov,* an opera by Modest Mussorgsky and the most recorded Russian opera. Interestingly Rimsky-Korsakov and Dimitri Shostakovich created new versions of this opera to correct weaknesses they saw in the original score. These were popular for decades but the revisions have now fallen out of favour.

I was still involved with *Can Can* and performing *The Merry Widow* once a week in Munich so it was a very busy time for both of us.

The Count of Luxembourg was lots of fun. Because of Jon's other commitments, I sometimes performed with another lead tenor. A colleague of ours, who had her entrance after one of our duets, reminded me a couple of years later that I had insisted she come on stage straight away, during the last bar of the duet, while the other tenor was my partner. On the other hand, when Jon and I were performing, she wasn't allowed to make a move until the applause had finished. We needed time for a kiss at the end of the duet.

Jon signed a contract for Siegmund and Siegfried in a new production of Wagner's *Ring* with the English National Opera. This was something Jon had wanted for a while. It was very exciting and challenging. A big task. Every spare moment he had, he spent on the

Ring. The English National Opera sent over a repetiteur to Kiel. He stayed a week at a time and whenever Jon had a break from other rehearsals, they got together and worked furiously. I don't know how his vocal folds didn't go on strike. Jon also worked with our favourite coach, Annie, who had all the Wagner experience he was looking for.

The Count of Luxembourg, Kiel, 1970

Jon was working on Siegmund in English. At the same time he was rehearsing the same part in German for a new production in Kiel, due to commence on 9 April. He was also singing in performances of *Luxembourg*, *Boris Gudonov* and *Fidelio*. How did he do it? His stamina was quite amazing.

To keep myself occupied during the last months in Kiel, I accepted an offer to sing Venus in *Orpheus in the Underworld*. The music for this, the first classical full-length operetta, was written by Jacques Offenbach. It was first performed in 1858 in France. Until then France had a law that did not allow certain genres of full-length works.

Offenbach based the story on Greek mythology and made a scathing satire of Gluck and his *Orfeo ed Euridice*. The story culminates in the Infernal Galop (can-can) that shocked some in the audience at the premiere. I had performed the parts of both Euridice and Venus in Sweden a couple of years earlier so I thought it would be reasonably easy. A week before the first dress rehearsal, I began to worry as nobody had spoken to me about costumes. Every time I asked the designer he told me not to worry. Everything was going to be fine.

Finally, I went to the costume people and told them I wanted to see my costume.

'What costume?' was their reaction. 'You're not having a costume!'

Were they joking? No, they were serious. The designer had decided that Venus should be naked. My response would have cracked your eardrums. Somebody, who obviously was not scared of hysterical women, suggested that rather than talking to them I should talk to the designer. The designer had been involved in a motorbike accident and was in an intensive care unit at the hospital. I was so angry that as I drove myself to the hospital I told myself that this was the best place for him to be at the moment. A couple of nurses unsuccessfully tried to stop me from entering the room where the man was lying in pain. I did not leave his room until he promised to design a costume for Venus. He did have a dress made in a material that looked normal but under the spotlight became transparent. I wore enough stuff underneath the dress to keep me warm while skiing! Who did he think he was dealing with?

Jon, Rick and I left Kiel and headed for Augsburg at the beginning of June. The rehearsals for *The Gypsy Baron*, in which we were the leading couple, started straight away and were quite an experience for me.

Music and Love

Jon and Monique in the lead roles in
The Gypsy Baron, Augsburg, 1971

Johann Strauss's *The Gypsy Baron* is known as a comic opera. I had my first rehearsal with Heinrich Hirsch, the conductor, and afterwards he took me aside and told me that he didn't think I was right for the part. The part of Saffi was written for a mezzo soprano, which I am not. Of course Hirsch was right. I say that now but at the time I felt totally numb and speechless. I muttered to myself, 'I'll show you!'

Heinrich Hirsch was a splendid person and conductor. The rehearsals went smoothly and Heinrich Hirsch didn't make any other frank or hurtful comments.

The Gypsy Baron was staged at the old City Wall. It is an open theatre connected to the Wall and is full of atmosphere. The opera house stages an open-air summer festival with two productions every year in this magic place. I loved the role of Saffi, both musically and emotionally, and was determined to prove Heinrich Hirsch wrong. The premiere went very well and I could see Heinrich Hirsch actually smiling in the pit! Afterwards, the little man with the big heart and mind complimented me and apologised for having been so totally wrong. Now that is greatness!

Another memorable experience with this wonderful conductor happened during the first dress rehearsal of *A Night in Venice.* This was also in Augsburg at the opera house itself. Heinrich Hirsch approached me one day before the rehearsals began with some sheet music in his hands. It was 'The Tipsy Song', which doesn't appear in the score of *A Night in Venice,* but was later added on by Johann Strauss. Hirsch suggested strongly that he would be very happy if

I would have a look at it and add it to the rest of my songs in the operetta. I did have a look and became terrified. At that point of my career, I had never been 'tipsy' or even 'funny' on stage, and the thought of it really scared me. But there is always a first time and I liked the challenge. I remember how fearful I felt, standing in the wings, ready to walk out on stage for 'The Tipsy Song'. I was close to tears.

The time came. There was a feeling of unreality, as if I were sleep-walking on stage and hearing myself singing. It is not the normal thing to look directly at the conductor. Normally one can see their movements out of the corner of one's eye. I suddenly became aware of a black hole, where the conductor should be. I looked down into the pit and saw there was no conductor. Somehow I kept singing and I could hear and see the whole orchestra following me. They were all standing up and accompanying me. There was a huge applause at the end of the song, not just from the audience but also from the orchestra.

It seems the conductor realized, after a couple of bars, that none of the orchestra were looking at him but were standing up, following me directly. So, Heinrich Hirsch just sat down and let the orchestra do it their way. I don't know one other conductor who would have behaved like that.

From that moment on, 'The Tipsy Song' has been my signature melody. Thank you, Heinrich Hirsch.

Monique singing 'The Tipsy Song', A Night in Venice, Augsburg, c. 1972

Chapter Five

Music is eternal – only hearing is intermittent.
Henry David Thoreau

Australia

Jon and I had an invitation from ABC TV to make a television series in Melbourne, entitled 'Monique & Jon'. We were booked on a flight on 2 August 1971. Late in July, my sister Rose Marie rang and told me that our Dad was sick and in hospital. They did not tell me just how sick he was.

I was able to book a return flight for Jon and myself to Gothenburg so we would be back in time to catch the plane to Melbourne. From the airport we went directly to the hospital, where I received a shock when I saw the shadow of what used to be my Dad. I was totally unprepared. Erik had cancer, which had spread all through his body. He took my hand and Jon's hand and asked if we were going to have children soon, whereupon I told him I was pregnant. My father's face broke into a wide smile. Jon's reaction was as extravagant as Dad's but for different reasons. Of course I wasn't pregnant. It just came out of my mouth without thinking, except that I understood it would make Dad happy. Looking at him, I could see he wouldn't be around long enough to find out the truth.

It all felt very surreal and traumatic to walk away from my father, waving and smiling knowing it could be the last time I would see him alive. This episode still troubles me in many ways. So many memories emerge and not all good. I have a memory as a desperate eleven-year old girl wondering what I could do to make Erik change his drinking habits, so that we could all have some peace.

I also remember as a seventeen-year-old being taken by the ear, and put over Erik's knee on the outside stairs to our house and given a hiding in front of our neighbours because I had gone for a ride on a motorbike. Not one person gave me any support.

In Erik's defence, seeing his daughter on a motorbike in the 1950s was the equivalent of seeing your teenage daughter taking drugs now. To him it was almost a criminal offence. The scene is imprinted on my memory but I believe there were other, less humiliating ways he could have dealt with my behaviour.

Jon and I did discuss the possibilities of cancelling arrangements in Australia, but no one in the hospital could tell us how long they thought Dad had left. Everyone tried to convince us he would still be around when we got back in about six weeks' time.

Of course they were wrong.

I have never become used to the awful length of time it takes to get to Australia. Even today I say, 'Never again!'

Despite our exhaustion, we arrived very happy and excited to be in Melbourne. We were welcomed by relatives and friends of Jon's, as well as the media.

One of the first questions to me was 'Where are you going to die?' Before Jon had time to translate the Australian accent, I answered, 'Well, probably in Sweden.' The response was, 'But you've just arrived from Sweden.' Bemused, I turned to Jon. Jon spoke perfect Oxford English. He repeated the question in my ear: 'Where are you going today?' I had never heard an Australian accent before.

This was a taste of what was in store for me in the coming weeks. Melbourne in the early 1970s was a city that was alive during the daytime but after 6.00 pm there was hardly anyone in the street.

The centre of the city was mostly occupied by business. There were no high-rise apartment blocks. Instead people lived in the suburbs, in private houses, which made Melbourne a huge city. It could take about an hour and a half to drive from one side of the city to the other. What interested me most was how every house was unique and not like any other house in the same street. It was so different to the European way.

What did not impress me was that the houses were not insulated. For a start, I don't think I've ever been as cold as those first two weeks in Melbourne. Despite having my fur coat with me, I was shivering. It was winter, but I grew up at the North Pole, so I'm not a stranger to cold. The only explanation I can come up with is, that perhaps the damp air from the south made the cold more penetrating.

We stayed with Ivy, a friend of Jon's mother and we were very well looked after. But it was hard to get out of bed in the mornings, especially as the toilet was outside.

I had a most wonderful time during this first visit to Australia, getting to know all the people close to Jon. I had heard so much about them all. I felt as if I already knew Jon's wonderful loving mother and his sweet and funny son Jon from his earlier marriage. I was also introduced to his friends Keith, Cath and Lorna.

We had some free time before the rehearsals and filming started at the ABC, so we drove north along the fantastic coastline of Victoria and New South Wales, ending up at Port Stephens. I certainly didn't need my fur coat there. We were introduced to Henry and Marcia Reid who became really good friends.

Being European, it was amazing to walk on a huge beach all by myself. I loved it. There is also something about the air and the sunlight in Australia. Whenever I come back and step out of the plane I am hit by the 'white' sunlight so different to our European sunshine.

I was invited to an Australian football match and this must be one of the most exuberant sporting events I have ever experienced.

Five minutes of this wild animal energy, sportsmanship and fun, and I was hooked – and this from someone who has not got the slightest interest in sport.

The production staff at the ABC was all very nice and professional. The director, Fred Maxian, was from Austria and was fascinated with operetta. He was very happy about us agreeing to perform some well-known operetta duets. All was not plain sailing, however.

The number one women's magazine in Australia is *The Women's Weekly* and they sent a journalist for an interview with us one morning before filming began. Because we were running late, the interview took place in the make-up room. We had quite a long chat and towards the end the journalist asked me if I had any pets and what were they called. I explained to her that my cat had a spot on its neck, hence its name 'Prick'. Jon shook his head and walked out. That is when I realized the *faux pas* I had made. I quickly explained that 'prick' is 'spot' in Swedish. To emphasize the difficulty with language I gave her other examples such as 'cunt' which means 'edge' in Swedish, and 'cock' which means 'cook', in Swedish.

The article was never published. What a total waste of time! Apart from some linguistic difficulty the time at the ABC was fun.

The series wasn't shown until some months later and we were told it was a great success.

Before we left Melbourne, something strange happened. The neighbour next door to Ivy with whom we were staying used to sit on a bench outside his front door reading a book almost every day. One day he wasn't there and Ivy told us he had suddenly passed away on 9 September. We all attended his funeral on 13 September. I was overcome with emotion at his funeral. A week later I had a letter from my sister, with the news that my father passed away on 9 September and his funeral was planned for 13 September.

Our departure from Melbourne was quite sad, but we all tried to be as brave as we could. We made Jon's Mum promise she would come to Germany and visit us as soon as she could and we of course also promised to return when possible.

ABC TV series, 'Monique & Jon', 1971

Chapter Six

Learn from other people's mistakes.
You won't live long enough to make them all yourself.

Germany, 1971–74

Rehearsals for *Land of Smiles* began in Augsburg as soon as we got back from Australia and kept us busy for a while. We also moved in to a new apartment which Ricky, our cat, didn't really enjoy that much. Like most cats, Ricky was an indoor cat. He was only taken outside once for a photo shoot in Kiel and this ended up with blood running down Jon's face. I've never seen a cat with claws as long as Ricky's. I don't think we ever thought of cutting them.

Lisa in *Land of Smiles* is one of the roles I've really enjoyed singing. Somehow every bar of music felt as if it was written for my voice. This is an indescribably wonderful feeling for a singer. The character of Lisa was also interesting and most of the time I've enjoyed playing this part.

The opera house engaged a well-known guest tenor for Jon's role, Prince Sou Chong, when Jon had to go to London for performances. This artist was the most adored leading tenor in Germany from the 1950s to the 1970s and had made more recordings than any other classical singer during that period. It was quite an honour to share the stage with this legend.

Jon and Monique in the lead roles, *Land of Smiles,* Augsburg, 1972

We were a little worried as we knew he had been driving by himself from Italy but happily he arrived in time. The rehearsal went quickly and easily and we got ready for the performance. The star's dresser was placed in the wings during the whole of the performance with a glass of champagne, which the tenor drank whenever there was a convenient moment.

The tenor and I were finishing one duet and during the very end of the last tone, my partner threw his mouth into my face while I was still producing the top note with my mouth wide open. My teeth came together in less than a thousandth of a second. I cannot tell you if any blood spurted out from the tenor's tongue. I was too agitated to notice. I wish there was a film of the event as I would love to know what the audience saw.

I had been told that about a hundred female admirers constantly travelled with the star to all of his performances. I didn't believe this until I actually saw them with my own eyes. I could not avoid seeing them as they blocked the entrance to the stage door and no one could get out.

Besides the leading tenor roles in Wagner's *Der Fliegende Holländer* and the world premiere of Alejandro Vinao's *Rashamon*, Jon also appeared together with me in *Show Boat* and this was a lot of fun. We both knew the English version so well, that it became quite comical sometimes, when we heard ourselves delivering the dialogue in German.

Every year, in the week before Ash Wednesday a Lenten festival called Fasching or Fastnacht is celebrated in the southern part of Germany. It involves lots of outdoor festivities and parades. At this time of the year the audience is allowed to throw buns on stage during performances. So far I have not heard of any singer choking on a bun during an aria.

Show Boat was performed during Fasching in 1972. I did not get a bun in my face but think I would have preferred a bun to what actually happened. At one stage during the performance, my character, Magnolia, had to perform an audition. I had played this part hundreds of times in Sweden and I wanted to do lots of things differently. The audition was one example. I rather liked the idea of accompanying myself on a guitar. Unfortunately I don't play the guitar but that didn't stop me. I grabbed one of the musicians in the orchestra and begged him to teach me four or five chords. He happily agreed. I was pleased with myself and keen to go on stage with my guitar and my few chords. I thought it sounded quite good.

The guitar was sitting in the wings waiting for me. The moment came for the audition so I grabbed the guitar and sailed out on stage. 'Bang!' I hit the first chord. Someone had loosened all the strings and the guitar was unplayable. There was nothing I could do but keep going 'a capella' as if the guitar was just an ornament hanging on my arm. I don't know even now who was to blame for what happened. Was it jealousy, or maybe just a bad joke?

It is so easy to catch a cold, as we all know. A cold for a singer is like breaking a leg for a dancer. Most of the time the performance has to be cancelled and the opera house must find a replacement artist as quickly as possible. It is a routine exercise and we are all used to it.

One of the worst guest performances I've ever experienced was when I had to step into a performance of *The Merry Widow* in Frankfurt. A rehearsal with the conductor involved running through the most important phrases, where he pointed out when to stay on a certain note, and when to just keep going. This is very important. If you are not together with the orchestra you will make a fool of yourself. The first performance arrived. Every note I had been told to hold for a while, the orchestra did not. Every note I had been told to just keep going, the orchestra stopped.

I heard afterwards that the conductor was having a relationship with the soprano who I was replacing. Was it deliberate sabotage? I can only suspect but never know for sure.

One positive aspect of this production was that my leading man was Erland Hagegård, a lovely Swedish baritone. In spite of the musical disaster, we had lots of fun together on stage. I remember having to turn my back to the audience at one point to stifle hysterical laughter at hearing the two of us, both Vikings, communicating in North Pole German.

Jon had a cousin, Ken Neate, who also happened to be a splendid Heldentenor, and had sung in all the big opera houses around the world. He was about twenty years older than Jon, and World War II was not just a tragedy for the world but affected Ken's career. He felt he had to stop his engagements and join the army. I had never met Ken until one day Jon received a phone call from him. The next thing I remember is the doorbell ringing. I opened the door and saw a big, happy-looking Aussie with a large bag of tomatoes in his arms. He proceeded to inform me that he could only stay for a week. Those tomatoes were very precious to Ken. No breakfast without his tomatoes!

It was great for all of us having found each other. Ken was a wonderful singer and, with his long experience, particularly in the Wagnerian repertoire, Jon could not have asked for a better coach. Of course I also took advantage of having a first-class singing teacher living with us. Munich had become Ken's home town and he stayed there for the rest of his life. I think he had always been single, but to our big surprise he announced when he was almost seventy that he was going to marry Gertrude Vollardt, a singer colleague. Gertrude was an Austrian mezzo who had been performing in one of Ken's last productions.

Life was very pleasant. Every free day gave Jon time to focus and concentrate on both the English and German version of the *Ring* cycle. He had also been engaged for a new production of the *Ring* in Leipzig. I really do not know how he pulled it off. Just learning a small part from the *Ring* in one language would have given me grey hair. To learn the huge roles of both Siegfried and Siegmund in two languages at the same time was unbelievable.

Australian humour can seem very harsh, and can also be difficult to appreciate if you have a European background. One day, when Jon and I had lunch in the Green Room with our colleagues in the opera house, one of the men with whom we had a close friendship said he had something he just had to tell us. After he'd told us his story both Jon and I just shook our heads.

Our friend informed us, that about one month after Jon and I had started our engagements in Augsburg, all the male singers in the opera house had a meeting to discuss how they could punish Jon and teach him how to treat his wife. They discussed taking him outside after a performance and giving him a real hiding. This did not happen, and they were all thankful later when they got to know Jon and his Australian humour a little better. They were shocked at the way Jon addressed me, with comments such as 'Come on, fatty.' Deep down, I must admit, I felt honoured that people actually cared, even though it was totally unnecessary.

Jon as *Siegmund*, Leipzig, 1974

Jon as *Siegfried*, Leipzig, 1974

This baritone friend also happened to be interested in numbers and astrology. He told us one day that he was going to shorten his life on a certain day after his sixty-fifth birthday because it was indicated astrologically. We later got a 'last letter' from him and then got the message he had actually taken his life on that specific date.

How intelligent people can be involved with absolutely unthinkable actions because of extreme beliefs sickens me. This same friend used to tell us about the thousands and thousands of Russian tanks sitting along the border between East and West Germany, and that it was just a question of a year, maybe months, before the Russians would take over the whole of the Western World.

I was in Germany in 1989 when the Wall fell. I thought about our friend, and wished I had had the courage, fifteen years earlier, to tell him my thoughts and perhaps have made him reconsider his decision based solely on numbers!

When it came to transport, Jon was the designated driver. I never touched the steering wheel, to Jon's relief. But I was in for a surprise. I arrived home from rehearsals one day and sitting parked outside our apartment was a cute little red VW. As we walked past it, Jon put some keys in my hand and told me to try it out. I loved the car, but I had no intention of driving it until I was by myself and had no witnesses to any embarrassing mistakes I might make.

My mother came for a visit a couple of days later and she had the honour of being the first passenger on my first trip in the new car. I had not driven a car for a long time and so was quite nervous. While getting into the car, I explained to my mother that I was going to drive straight forward all the time – no lefts or rights. I didn't care where we ended up. I planned to take a taxi back from wherever we finished up when I thought it was time to stop. I continued driving forward for what seemed like a lifetime, when I suddenly recognized our house in front of us. I'm not sure how this was possible. Jon was quite impressed as he knew I had no sense of direction.

For years I had been troubled by inflamed tonsils. When it became obvious that they were chronically infected, I was advised to have them removed in case I developed blood poisoning. One of my female colleagues at the opera house had her tonsils out by a throat specialist in Starnberg. He only handled singers and people who didn't want to hurt their voices. My friend explained the procedure to me, in detail, and so by the time I attended my first appointment with this genius I felt I knew exactly what to expect.

The surgeon did not use full anaesthesia with his patients so that it was not necessary to put anything down their throat that could damage the vulnerable vocal folds. The procedure took place under local anaesthesia. I was tied to a chair, with a nurse firmly holding my head to stop the slightest unexpected movement that could have upset the surgery.

Suddenly I could not breathe!! I felt the panic rising. There was no way I could alert them as my vocal folds didn't work because of the local anaesthetic and my legs and arms were tied to a chair. I was helpless! After what seemed like an eternity the surgeon noticed the panic in my eyes and paused. What had happened was that blood from the incisions had run into my windpipe. He stuck two long tongs full of cotton down my throat and cleaned out the blood. This was in the early 1970s, and no doubt techniques have improved.

In spite of the unexpected drama I was very happy to get rid of the two tennis balls in my throat and the operation solved the problem. The timbre of my voice did not seem to have been affected either. This is one of the reasons many singers are concerned about throat surgery.

When Melba developed a nodule on her left vocal cord in 1890, no surgical operation existed to help her other than complete rest for the voice. Even then a cure could not be guaranteed. Fortunately, months of rest restored Melba's voice to its normal beauty.

In 1972, the year of the Munich Olympics I was involved because *The Merry Widow* was one of the cultural happenings planned during the big event. We lived in Augsburg. This isn't very far from Munich, and the autobahn between the two cities passes the Olympic Stadium area. I happened to have the radio on while driving to Munich for the performance of the Widow. As I passed the stadium, I heard the announcement of a terror attack. I was shocked by the hysteria in their voices and knew something terrible must have happened. I had no idea what to do, so kept on driving. There was total chaos at the opera house.

On 5 September, eleven Israeli athletes were taken hostage by Palestinian terrorists, armed with machine guns and grenades, who climbed up the wall of the Israelis' quarters. Two people were killed in the initial attack. The nine remaining hostages were later killed during a botched rescue attempt at a nearby airport.

The first thing to happen was a change of repertoire for the night. Instead of *The Merry Widow* it was decided that we would perform *Land of Smiles,* as this was the only operetta in the repertoire that has a sad ending. I have no idea how the total change of scenery, performers, costumes and all that went with it, was managed but it was. Driving past the stadium after the performance was emotional and very scary.

Living in the south of Germany gives you the feeling that you are close to most places in Europe, and Jon and I took the opportunity to travel around as soon as we were free to do so. We spent lots of time in our favourite places such as Venice, Vienna, and Salzburg. I was eager to go on a skiing holiday in the Austrian alps during winter, but had been unable to convince Jon to be part of it.

The reason for Jon's lack of enthusiasm was not just that we had signed contracts that did not allow any adventures that could endanger health. I believe the reason for Jon's hesitation was most likely due to the fact that he had never had skis on his feet and therefore was not an experienced skier.

I could hardly believe my ears when one day Jon suggested we drive up to Hochgurgl, a ski resort in Austria, the following weekend. It was mid-January 1973 and there was lots of snow up in the mountains. The views on the way were compelling despite the tricky driving conditions. As soon as we had unpacked and had lunch we set off to hire our skis and a ski instructor for Jon.

With extreme difficulty Jon was at last able to put on his skis. As he had chosen an uphill position to do this it was little short of a miracle that he did eventually get them on. The following picture is imprinted on my brain.

Very slowly he began to move down the hill backwards. As he passed a crowd of dumbfounded skiers waiting for the lifts, he endeavoured to put on a facial expression to indicate that he was enjoying showing off a new routine that had never been seen before. He slid slowly backwards until he ended up on his back, utterly helpless, with no idea how to get up or get the skis off his feet. He waited desperately for me to come and save him from further embarrassment, since without help he would have been there for a long, long time.

It was then time for the ski lesson. Unfortunately the instructor's English was not very good and a frustrated Jon told him to depart in no uncertain terms. Jon then angrily turned around and lost control. The skis took him down a long and steep hill until he fell like a log. A local doctor declared that nothing was broken, although there was no doubt he was going to be very, very sore.

Back in the hotel, I left Jon sitting in a warm bath soothing his aching limbs while I had a swim in the pool. When I returned to our room, I expected Jon to be asleep and I was correct, except he was asleep in the bath with the tap running. I was speechless, and could not work out how the bathroom floor was not flooded. As I helped Jon crawl out of the bath, he said he had never been so exhausted in his life. He could not even find the strength to reach over and turn off the water. However, he felt the plug under his bottom and managed to remove it so at least the water was able to drain out.

We were left with one big problem: a reason to give the opera house for cancelling Jon's performances and rehearsals for at least one week. Jon received sympathy from everyone when they were told his pathetic story about falling down the stairs in the apartment house and bruising all his ribs.

Chapter Seven

Music is enough for a lifetime, but a lifetime is not enough for music.
Sergei Rachmaninoff

Developments in Germany

Summer arrived and I had a break. For Jon it was as busy as usual, as he had performances in London. He loved it. I had a wonderful time attending different performances each day. London was then the place to be, if your big love was the theatre.

Making his debut as Siegmund in the English National Opera's production of Wagners's *Die Walküre* was one of the most important events in Jon's career and he was fantastic. The newspapers agreed with me.

Two friends visited us from Australia during the summer and we lent them our little VW to drive around and see as much as possible of Europe. They came with me to the dress rehearsal of *Die Walküre* and Henry found this to be one of the most effective sleeping pills he had ever come across. Henry produced a snoring sound that nearly drowned out the orchestra. I must admit that I needed a couple of years myself before I truly appreciated Wagner.

Jon and I had now been married for over four years and I had never before been as happy. A new feeling started to grow inside me. This was the longing for a child. At first I dismissed the idea but it didn't take long before the feeling took over too strongly to be denied.

Music and Love

I had to have a baby. London has always had some magic power over my life. That is where I first heard Jon's voice, got married and now it was time to make a baby a reality. I became pregnant and during the pregnancy we referred to the growing baby as Debbie. Nine months later Jon brought me to a hospital in Hammersmith for the birth of our beloved child – a boy!

Jon as Siegmund in *Die Walküre*, London, 1974

But lots of things were to happen before that.

We returned as usual to Germany in August, this time to the city of Essen, where I had signed a one-year contract. We had not told Ricky, our cat, as we knew it would upset him madly to have to move again. Two colleagues from Augsburg who had looked after Ricky while we were away told us nervously one day that they loved him and wished he could stay with them. We knew we would miss him, but also knew he could not be in a better home with people that loved him. We both shed tears driving away from him. We were comforted by the knowledge that if we missed him too badly, we could take him home again.

I had just started the engagement in Essen, when it became obvious that 'Debbie' was alive and well. 'She' told me at just four weeks of age but I knew she was alive after just one minute's existence. I have never felt as physically well and psychologically strong as during the next eight months. I have often said I wish I was constantly pregnant as I felt so good. I rang Jon immediately with the news. He was back in London for more performances so we had a crazy celebration over the phone.

It was now up to me to give the opera house the big news. Dr Schuhmacher, a former SS general, was the intendant of the Essen Opera House, and the man I had to approach. I made an appointment and told him the news politely and then walked away with my head held high. I did not turn my head so I could not see his facial expression. There was no screaming or abuse, although I had been warned this happened on a daily basis. I told myself that perhaps Dr Schuhmacher loved little babies.

Mr Fechner, Dr Schuhmacher's assistant, later requested that I write down the practical details concerning the expected birth date so that they could begin to organize 'stand ins' for my performances.

Everyone in the Opera House in Munich was happy for me when I told them the news. I felt sure I would only have to cancel my performances for the two months before and after the birth.

The people in the opera house in Kiel, who regarded Jon and myself as 'theirs' were absolutely delighted by the news. I was still performing in *The Gypsy Princess* with them and promised to keep going until February 1974, two months before the birth.

Our stay in Essen was a bit over two years, but I never felt quite at home in this opera house, although I formed a lovely friendship with Maggie Turner, a wonderful Australian soprano and her husband, Joggie. They later became our main babysitters.

My first production in Essen was *Land of Smiles*, which I knew backwards. The rehearsals went smoothly and I felt fantastic all the time. We received an excellent response from the audience and from the newspapers after the premiere. Everyone was happy, even Dr Schuhmacher. So much for the premiere.

The dress rehearsal, on the other hand, had been a real disaster. As the saying goes, if the dress rehearsal is bad, then the premiere will be a success.

During my professional life most designers have been happy with me as somehow I always fitted into whatever design they came up with. The opera house was broke and tried to find old costumes in the 'Fundus' from earlier productions that they could change and use again. The opening of *Land of Smiles* takes place at Lisa's (my role) birthday party. Lisa is from a middle-class Viennese family and a lady. I was given something to wear that you wouldn't give a cat. We got through the first act and Elisabeth, my dresser, and I had a rest in my dressing room. There was a bang on the door and before I had time to react, Dr Schuhmacher marched in.

'Well done, Miss Brynnel, but I would appreciate it if you behaved and looked more like a lady on stage.'

I pulled myself up to my full height and replied furiously. 'How dare you come in to my dressing room like this! If anyone in this opera house knows how to behave like a lady, it is I! I suggest for a start that you get me something lady-like to wear, and then we can talk about being lady-like. Now – please leave my dressing room!'

Off he went. Elisabeth, my friend and dresser, had sunk to the floor crying, 'Oh, my God! Oh, my God!'

This is the first and only time in my life that I can remember being really angry, and having the courage to express it. I can only put it down to hormonal changes brought on by my pregnancy.

We all went through the second act without any problems and I returned quite happily to my dressing room after the last curtain call. I was half-naked when I heard a little scratch on the door. I called out 'Just a moment', slipped on my robe, opened the door and a little mouse crept in.

'I am so sorry, dear Miss Brynnel, for having treated you so badly in the interval. Please forgive me. And, by the way, you were marvellous. Thank you so much!' Dr Schuhmacher slunk out before I had the chance to tell him he was allowed to leave.

Out of all the people employed at the opera house, there was only one, as far as I know, who Dr Schuhmacher addressed in a polite and respectful way and that was – me! I don't believe anyone spoke to him the way he addressed people himself. It may have been a first for him at the opera house.

I had reached a new chapter of my life, where some things were worth fighting for – thanks to 'Debbie'.

Jon was now totally focused on his Heldentenor repertoire. This gave him enormous inspiration, but was also stressful. Even when stressed it is possible to pull off a performance like *Land of Smiles* with a bit of a cold. But a little bit of a cold can be a big monster if you have a hugely complex part like Siegmund or even Florestan, both vocally demanding roles. The Heldentenor is a rarity with a large voice and baritonal quality and has a well-developed middle and low register. The Fach is the dividing line between the lyric and dramatic tenor voice.

Sometimes Jon suffered from all sorts of allergies that made his nose run and caused lots of sneezing. This was very unsettling and worrying for him. He never knew when an allergy would occur. He always seemed to sail through in spite of some difficult times, such as having to mime a dress rehearsal of *Die Walküre* with someone else singing from the pit.

Performing together had its pluses and minuses. When performing without Jon, I was more able to focus just on my own performance. When we were together on stage, I was more focused on what Jon did. The big minus of not performing together was, of course, that we had to spend lots of time away from each other. Nothing in life is perfect. We were still so lucky and had so much to be thankful for.

The autumn of 1973 was as busy as ever. The difference for me with being pregnant was that I felt incredibly energetic and strong. When I wasn't performing in Essen, I was on stage either in Kiel or Munich.

Jon had been invited to record the sound-track of a new opera, *Violins of St Jacques,* that ABC television was filming in Melbourne in November and December. Unable to join him, I remained in Germany by myself. There were no computers or mobile phones and communication still relied on the postman. Our phone had not been connected in our newly built house. When Jon's first letter arrived with a tape recording inside, I was frantic when I couldn't get our tape recorder to work. I drove to a park nearby and used the recorder in the car. I listened to his voice with tears pouring down my face. They do say pregnant women are emotional.

If a performer has a nightmare, it nearly always involves something going wrong in the theatre.

One Sunday evening while Jon was in Australia, I was sitting in my pyjamas, relaxing and enjoying a free evening in front of the television. It was about five to seven. There was a frantic knocking on the door. I opened it to find the stage manager from the opera house.

'What's going on?' I asked

'The performance is starting in five minutes!' he yelled

'What performance?'

'*Land of Smiles*, of course!' he replied, frantically helping me into my coat. I was confused, muttering, 'This is mad. I have no performance. They are crazy.'

The drive normally took about fifteen minutes from our place to the theatre. We arrived after seven minutes at the stage door where about twenty people from the ensemble were standing looking somewhat hysterical. I was the only calm person around. When they saw me stepping out of the car they began to laugh. I was still in my pyjamas. The stage manager told the audience that the performance was going to commence in five minutes. That was all the time I had to get ready.

Impossible! Totally impossible! I dragged on my dreadful first costume before I walked up twenty stairs backstage for my first entrance, singing an aria while walking elegantly down the twenty stairs onto the stage. In the middle of the aria the heel on one of my shoes caught on something in the staircase and I began rolling down the stairs. I just kept rolling trying to look as if it was meant to be like that. There was panic in the chorus as they all knew I was four months pregnant at this time and they came rushing, prepared to carry me off.

I pulled myself up, finished my aria and left the stage. I had a break of about ten minutes before my next entrance. Shaking my head I said to Elisabeth, my dresser, 'After this, what else could happen? It can't get worse.' But I was wrong.

I walked onto the stage to begin the dialogue with my leading man. He looked different and in fact he was different. Nobody had thought to tell me that our usual tenor was sick and that a substitute had to be found. Every move this poor person made was different from our production. If I turned to the left he would be to the right, behind me, and the other way round.

It was truly a nightmare!

I still don't know how I could possibly have made such an error. I always kept a list with all the dates of my performances stuck on the fridge. Somehow this one got lost.

Despite the trauma, I have to be thankful that nothing dramatic happened while falling down the stairs. Not even a scratch.

Chapter Eight

Share your dreams and see them grow.

To London again – and Jack!

Jon arrived back just in time to celebrate our fifth Christmas together, and it looked as if it was going to be the last one for just the two of us.

The Gypsy Princess, Kiel, 1974

I performed the last *Gypsy Princess in Kiel* on 24 January and we left for London on 16 February. We moved in to a lovely house in St. Mary's Grove, where I felt at home immediately. The Underground was just a couple of minutes walk away, so I could take myself into the city very quickly if I needed to. Jon was busy with rehearsals at the English National Opera as usual, and was due to commence a short tour with *Die Walküre* a couple of weeks later.

Before we left Germany, I contacted the Swedish Embassy in Hamburg to get some information regarding a good obstetrician in London, and was given the name of one in Harley Street. My first appointment to see him was at the end of February. A very smart-looking gentleman in an evening suit greeted me. He did not seem interested in performing the usual checks like urine and blood tests, but talked about the weather and the news of the day. I was bewildered when I left his rooms as something did not feel right. I rang the obstetrician's secretary as soon as I got home, and told her I would like to see the premises where I was to deliver my baby. She organized a time for me the following day.

When Jon and I walked into the delivery rooms, we looked at each other and left as quickly as we could. The delivery room in the clinic was like something out of a Dickens novel. In shock, and outraged, I rang the Swedish Embassy. I told them what had happened and asked for an explanation. They told me it was difficult for women to get an abortion in Sweden at that time and thousands of Swedish women took 'abortion holidays' in London. The person at the Embassy had evidently thought I was one of these women and was happy to help out.

We turned to our friend Alfred Alexander who had his surgery in Harley Street not far from the abortion clinic, and asked him for help.

He referred me to Dr Robinson, an obstetrician with rooms next door to him. I could not have wished for a more caring and knowledgeable person to be with me during our baby's birth.

There must have been something in the water during the summer of 1973. My sister Rose Marie and my good friend Lena in Kiel both became pregnant at the same time as I did. I rang Lena shortly after I arrived in London to see how things were going. Her husband Ernst answered the phone and told me that he had taken Lena to the hospital the night before. She was two months early but that wasn't the only surprise. When the nurses started to clean up after the birth of the baby, Lena made a strange noise and out popped baby number two. It was a baby girl who had kept her presence a secret for about seven months by hiding under her sister every time Lena had an ultrasound or check-up with the doctor.

Rose Marie delivered her beautiful little boy about two weeks before it was my turn. Everything went as expected for Rose Marie and having a leading obstetrician as a husband was added insurance.

Our little baby was determined to keep us guessing whether it was a boy or a girl. The baby managed to be lying in a position that prevented anyone from recognizing its gender. The sex of our baby remained a secret to everyone except us. We had decided all along that it was a girl.

The day of the birth came closer and closer. I don't know how other women experience pregnancy, but all I felt was total fulfillment and strength all the time. I did not prepare myself or worry greatly about how to look after a baby.

Nick Braithwaite was the conductor of *Die Walküre* and he has been a really good friend to us both ever since. At this time of his life he was single and spent many of his free days with us. Jon would make some gorgeous dinner, or we would go to a pub where the boys had beer. There was mineral water for the mother-to-be.

On 14 April, the day before the birth of the baby, Nick and I had a great time playing squash! I confess it was on a machine at the pub but Nick has entertained audiences with this memory.

I decided to be a good girl and not stay out too late, so the boys took me home for an early night. A couple of hours later I woke up believing I had wet the bed. Then it hit me. My membranes had ruptured. The baby was coming!

Monique with Nicholas Braithwaite, one day before Jack was born

I told Jon what had happened. He turned around and told me not to be stupid. When I screamed at him he realized I was serious. Half asleep, he drove me to the hospital in Hammersmith.

I didn't have any pain or discomfort but couldn't stop shaking. I felt at that moment as if I had been asleep for nine months and had suddenly woken up under a cold shower as reality hit me. Our child was about to be born. Dr Robinson came and checked and was sure it was going to take quite some time before the delivery would begin.

I remember Jon coming back a bit later and sharing a bottle of champagne with the nurses. Jon was able to rest in one of the empty rooms. After about twenty hours the pains really started and I was given an epidural injection. Four hours later our beautiful baby was born! Jon had his tape recorder with him in the delivery room and at the moment of our child's birth you can hear Jon's voice: 'Oh, my God, IT'S A BOY!!'

So it was. Thank you, God, for our beautiful son, Jack!

He opened his eyes.

How long did our eyes speak to each other? What messages did our brains pick up? It was an eternity; everything still.

A sudden movement in his body made me bring him into my arms and gently to my breast. The child, who had lived in my inner thoughts for a long time and physically for nine months, was no longer a stranger. I felt I knew everything about him. Having shared our lives, I sensed his feeling of familiarity, and my vocal folds slowly started to vibrate and made a soft, to him recognizable, sound comforting him during his first feeding.

My son, Jack!

Trio

Chapter One

If children hear fine music from the day of their birth and learn how to play it, they develop mental sensitivity, discipline and endurance.
They get a beautiful heart...
Shin'ichi Suzuki

A new beginning!

The daily routine, as I had known it, changed overnight. I now had to be ready to feed at any time, communicate with unfamiliar words and sounds, change nappies and complete the myriad tasks required when looking after a new baby. I was also constantly checking that everything was under control.

What had I been doing for the last nine months? Had my brain been on holidays? A newborn child needs to be cared for twenty-four hours a day. I had not prepared myself for the role of mother or even thought about what would happen when the baby physically arrived into our world. I had been living in bliss for nine months, only aware that I was carrying a beautiful baby inside my body. I enjoyed no extra physical jobs or responsibilities.

I was in for a BIG surprise!

The newcomer became the most important member of the Weaving family from day one. Everything in our lives now rotated around this little angel's needs and habits.

Performances, rehearsals, needs for resting, eating times, our daily routine, everything became unimportant compared to the responsibility of looking after our little 'prince'.

I think someone might have whispered in our baby's ear that his Mum and Dad both liked to sleep in. I was definitely blessed in having a baby who had the same sleeping patterns as Jon and myself. I don't think I had to get up in the middle of the night once because there was a hungry baby crying for my attention.

We did not have other family members to advise us, and had not prepared adequately for the arrival of our child, or had prepared incorrectly with things like pink baby clothes. Jon's mother lived in Melbourne, and of course, my family was in Sweden. We had no one to share this time of our lives with or even turn to if we needed help or parenting advice.

For nine months we had been communicating with a baby called Debbie, convinced it would be a girl. We had no name planned for a boy. I could only think of a Swedish name Björn, and Jon came up with Weymouth, a name every male in the Weaving family is cursed to carry. None of them 'tasted' right. One day, out of the blue, I came up with Jack and Jack it was! It was 1974 and Jon had great difficulty persuading the Register Office to accept Jack as the real name for our son. We were told, 'Jack is not a name! That's why it cannot be registered. It has to be John.'

We persevered and eventually won the battle. I understand that our Jack is the first Jack in Great Britain to have his name officially registered as Jack!

Jack had a very unusual time as a newborn baby. Besides having to deal with an amateur mother, he also spent his first weeks of life at the Coliseum in London listening to Wagner's *The Ring of the Nibelung* up to four to six hours a day. I was and still am convinced that Jack enjoyed every minute of the grandiose music that he was introduced to during that time. The reason for these extraordinary musical experiences was that Jon had the dress rehearsals for both

Siegmund and Siegfried with the English National Opera and there was no way that I was prepared to miss attending them.

Advertising poster showing Jon in *Siegfried*, London, 1976

The conducting of the *Ring* was shared between two brilliant masters, Reginald Goodall and Sir Charles Mackerras. Jon was delighted to be singing with fellow Australian Charles Mackerras in the pit. There were many first-class singers in the cast, such as Rita Hunter, Ann Howard, Margaret Kingsley, Norman Bailey, Clifford Grant and Gregory Dempsey, to mention a few. The producers of the *Ring* were Glen Byam Shaw and John Blatchley, and the production was later praised not only by the audience but also by the press.

It was a very exhilarating experience to share this highlight of Jon's career as a Wagnerian tenor together with our little baby. The Coliseum seats over 2300 people. To sit in this huge space all by myself, with a baby in my arms, transported by the sound of the voices and instruments weaving together the wonderful music of Wagner was an experience never to be forgotten. I am sure Jack agrees. He did not make one disturbing noise while spending hours in my arms, surrounded by warm darkness and heavenly music.

He loves Wagner to this very day.

Chapter Two

Where words fail, music speaks.
Hans Christian Anderson

Greta

A couple of days after Jack's birth, I had a phone call from my mother, Greta, in Sweden. She was deeply touched to hear the news of her new grandchild's birth. Judging from the excitement in her voice, she was preparing to board a plane right away, heading for London, but fate said otherwise.

Greta was calling from a hospital bed in Gothenburg. She had been suffering from stones in her gallbladder for years, and had tried unsuccessfully to get rid of them by using alternative medicine. She was due to have an operation on the next day, 19 April.

The operation went well, but before the surgery Greta was mistakenly given low blood pressure tablets instead of high blood pressure tablets. This caused complications and she spent another couple of weeks in hospital. One morning she called me and said she was feeling very strange and was having difficulty speaking. I thought she was just exhausted after the operation.

The next day Greta had a severe stroke and lost consciousness.

Jack and I flew to Sweden a few days later. Such a sad turn of events. I had been dreaming of arriving in Gothenburg with my little baby, and celebrating the new member of the family with everyone.

Instead all my thoughts and energy were now focused on my mother's condition.

Greta did not look sick; she just looked as though she was sleeping. I was shocked when the doctor asked us not to wish for her to wake up. He explained that because she had been unconscious for quite a while, she would become a vegetable, never being able to leave her bed even if she did wake up. I totally disregarded his comment.

I had a tape recorder with me. I put earphones in Greta's ears and let her listen to the cello solos she loved and had played herself. Before leaving I asked one of the nurses to keep the tapes going for some hours.

The next day Greta regained consciousness! She was not a vegetable, but she was unable to speak or move the left side of her body. Six months later, after extensive rehabilitation, she moved back in to her house and lived another seventeen years by herself. She had a carer who helped with cleaning and food preparation for a couple of hours a day. Greta was a very strong woman but it is hard to imagine how she managed both physically and emotionally.

Greta never recovered her ability to speak, and so I never discovered if she would have preferred to have gone to heaven rather than spend her last seventeen years chained to a wheelchair, unable to communicate except through body, face and sign language. I wonder whether my wish for her to wake up was a selfish one, to save myself from feeling the grief of losing her.

Chapter Three

A bird does not sing because it has an answer.
It sings because it has a song.
Chinese proverb

Fellini and surgery

We thought we were clever and knew everything. When we left Essen in Germany in February we thought we understood that when we returned there would be three of us instead of two, and that things would be different. No big deal!

We didn't come back until June, five months later. My duties at the Opera House thankfully didn't start until August when the rehearsals for *The Count of Luxembourg* would commence, so I was able to focus happily on just being a mother for a little while.

All of our friends and colleagues were keen to meet the new member of our family. The new situation also meant that we needed some of our friends as babysitters now and then. That turned out to be no problem whatsoever. However, every time Jon and I arrived back home Jack did not seem to be the slightest bit happy about having us back. Sometimes I had the uncomfortable feeling that Jack was quite annoyed with us for turning up. It was as if he tried to tell us he preferred other people to us, or perhaps it was punishment for leaving him behind.

Jon had to go back to London for performances of the *Ring* almost once a week. He didn't mind the travelling at all. It was hard work but very exciting.

While in London he received a phone call one day from his agent asking him to come to their office. They wouldn't tell him what it was about, so he didn't think it was anything urgent. When he visited them some days later, he was informed that Mr Fellini, the Italian film director, was interested in engaging him for the lead role in the new film *Casanova*.

Jon was a great entertainer and loved a good joke. He thought this offer was one of the funniest things he had ever heard, and he told his agent so. The agent explained to Jon that Fellini was looking for a 'sexy' man in the music world and had studied hundreds of pictures and reviewed information about male singers from the opera world in London, New York, Milan and elsewhere.

Fellini had chosen Jon from this large field. One of the things that Fellini had taken for granted was that Jon, being an Australian, would be able to ride a horse. Jon had never been on a horse in his life.

He left the office, still laughing and told Fellini's representatives to inform Mr Fellini, that he must be 'out of his bloody mind' for wanting to engage an Aussie – and furthermore one who had no film experience – for the starring role. When Jon told me about the offer I told him he was an absolute idiot for throwing away such an unbelievable opportunity. Fellini obviously thought so too. The agent called a couple of days later to tell Jon that he had sent a message to Fellini repeating Jon's comment, word for word. The role of *Casanova* went to Donald Sutherland.

I awoke one night with a really bad stomach pain. It became so bad that I had to go to the hospital next day. I was x-rayed and an inflamed appendix was found to be the problem. I was shocked when the doctor informed me he needed to operate as soon as possible.

It was the end of September and I had two first nights coming up and another ten weeks after that filled with performances. I was not comfortable with the thought of informing the opera house that I would not be able to perform for another couple of weeks because I had had so much leave after Jack's birth. I told the hospital I had to postpone the operation till mid-December. I went home, leaving a very annoyed group of medics behind, unaware of the danger I was putting myself in. I was extremely lucky that the appendix did not burst during the following three months.

When I eventually had it removed, something happened during the surgery. I don't know what in fact happened; it was serious. A couple of hours after the operation, I experienced being in a long, dark tunnel with a bright light at the very end. As I advanced to the light, some force or energy halted me, and pushed me back into the tunnel.

From there, I felt I was under the ceiling in my room in the hospital looking down on my own body. I became aware of feeling very cold. A nurse entered the room, and I felt myself slipping back into my body, telling her I was freezing and needed more blankets.

A male nurse who had been assisting during the operation came to visit me. He asked if he could talk to me and my husband later on. He said something had happened during my operation. I never saw him again. I didn't know him or what his name was, so didn't know how to find him. Something had clearly happened, but what?

I remained in the hospital for another ten days. On the day before Christmas I was allowed to go home. It was the first time I had gotten up and was walking, and I became aware of a pain in the upper part of my left leg. Thinking nothing of it, I gladly went home.

After hugging my two boys at home, I made a call to my sister Rose Marie in Sweden to wish her and the family a Merry Christmas. Rose Marie's husband Mats, a doctor, answered the phone and I gave him all the news. During the conversation, I mentioned the pain in my leg. Mats insisted that I go back to the hospital immediately. I did not want to go back to the hospital. It was Christmas! My protests were ignored.

At the hospital, a deep vein thrombosis was diagnosed. Unaware of the seriousness of the situation, I demanded to be allowed to go home. I was given injections and ordered to return every day for further injections. This went on for another month. I had been told there was a chance the thrombosis could move to a more dangerous place in my body, which could endanger my life.

I remember lying in bed urging Jon to marry again if I were to die because Jack needed a mother. What amazes me, thinking back on that moment, is that I wasn't terrified, shocked, or even deeply sad. My reaction was quite matter-of-fact. I find it hard to understand how I could have been so calm about this alarming situation. . Now, years later, I find I become very worried and depressed easily when thinking about dramatic events that can happen in life.

I often think about the pressure that I placed upon my beloved husband, and I am deeply sad that we never talked about this later on. I would have loved him to know how much I loved him for having been by my side when I so needed it.

This was my first Christmas as a mother. Jack had started walking a couple of days before I had the operation, and from then on he rarely crawled. He was only eight months old. Writing about this, I have to admit I don't remember if our little boy was at all impressed or eager to open the boxes that were placed in his hands that Christmas.

What I do remember is that Jon and I were looking forward to a new year that would be full of happiness, love and good health.

Chapter Four

I've been told that Wagner's music is better than it sounds.
Mark Twain

The Ring, everywhere

For Jon, 1975 was to become one of the busiest 'Wagnerian' years. He continued performing the *Ring*, not just in London but also all over Germany, even in East Germany in the new successful production by Professor Herz in Leipzig. If I could ask Jon today what he considered to be his best year, I am sure he would say with a happy smile on his face that it was 1975.

Jon told me lots of amazing and almost unbelievable things that he was experiencing whenever he went to Leipzig. I had not spent a lot of time in East Germany, so I was quite eager to join him for a couple of days to see it all with my own eyes.

We arranged the trip for mid-February, when I had a free week from my own performances. The three of us headed off to Leipzig in the car. At the border the car was 'stripped' and long sticks were pushed into the petrol tank – the usual search for forbidden material.

Jon was booked into the hotel in Leipzig where he normally stayed. Jack and I were invited to stay with Uwe Wand, the Regi Assistant, who had become a close friend of Jon. One of his colleagues at the opera house invited us to have dinner at his home that evening. There were two children in the family, both young teenagers.

During the meal, the conversation suddenly became very serious. The host's wife expressed her worries about the future of their children. She went on to say that the most important thing in her life was working out a way to smuggle the children out of the East, even if this meant she would never see them again and even if it meant she ended up in prison. I almost choked on the food and didn't really know how to respond.

Uwe, who was also a dinner guest, expressed his worries later about this conversation. School children were told by the school authorities to keep their eyes and ears open at home and to report any remarks that could be thought of as against East German policy. All reports were rewarded, and families were frequently split apart.

I could not believe that any child would dream of wanting to be part of an action that would destroy their family. I know now that this did happen. Children were taught that the most important thing in their lives was the State, even more important than the welfare of their own family.

Jack and I were taken to Uwe's place, where he lived by himself in a small apartment. Although we were supposed to stay for three nights it ended up just being one! It was freezing in the apartment even though Uwe told me he had heated the place especially for Jack and me. Jack and I lay in our beds with all our winter clothing on and still we were so cold it was impossible to fall asleep. I cursed Jon who for some reason clearly believed we would prefer this to staying in a hotel. The first thing I did next morning was to rush to the hotel with Jack, where I demanded a room for us.

I felt deeply sorry for and worried about Uwe, living in such conditions. Many lived like this in the East at the time. We in the West did not know our own good fortune, having material wealth and no fear of the State. However, misunderstandings can arise. I remember an unusual experience with the West German police force in Essen one night.

My routine after I finished a performance at night was to rush home to my boys as quickly as I could. That meant that I jumped out of my costume and into my clothes, not bothering to take off my stage make-up. I ran to my car that was parked close to the stage door, hoping to avoid the public waiting for an autograph or a photo.

This particular night I was driving the normal route home through a park in the city. Out from behind a bush stepped a policeman, waving for me to stop. I was *not* going to stop! I was by myself; how was I supposed to know if he was a real policeman? So I put my foot on the accelerator.

Normally it took another ten minutes to get home. I probably made it in half that time, because I saw in the rear-vision mirror that the policeman was racing after me with the siren screaming. Well, a policeman's daughter is not that easy to catch, especially when she does not have her driver's licence with her!

I was focusing all my energy on wishing Jon to be outside with my driver's licence when I arrived home. Although he wasn't outside and he didn't have my driver's licence in his hand, he was sitting by an open window looking for me and wondering what the siren was about. I jumped out of the car, shouted at him to grab my driver's licence on my dressing table and throw it to me. He did!

My confrontation with the policeman took all of two minutes. Before he had a chance to open his mouth, I asked if he realized how frightening his behaviour had been, jumping out from the darkness in front of my car in the middle of the park. Before Jon had time to come out and join me the policeman left without having said a word. I don't know whether I intimidated him with my attitude, or could it have been all the layers of the stage make-up still shining on my face?

He didn't even ask to see my licence before he drove off.

In the middle of the year Jon's mother, Marg, came to Europe to visit, and it was such a thrill to have her with us. Meeting her grandson for the first time was the highlight of her trip. She also attended as many our performances as possible. We spent a couple of weeks in Sweden where we took the opportunity to have Jack christened while we were all together. Jack's godparents, Ingalill and Ralph, were also with us. Jack was already fourteen months old, running around and making jokes. It was funny to see him wearing long trousers, held by his godmother Ingalill as he struggled to avoid the wetting of his head.

Before I knew it, 1975 had come to an end. It had been a year filled with the blessings of being a mother and seeing our little child grow. I also found myself taught by my child to look at the world with new eyes. I was a very happy and lucky human being.

Jon, with his mother Marg and son Jack, 1975

We were to spend Christmas again in London and stayed as usual in the house in St Mary's Grove. Ingalill and Ralph came from Sweden to celebrate New Year with us. We were delighted to hear they were going to sell their house in Hollviken and move to Skanor, a couple of miles further away. We were delighted because we decided there and then to buy their house and move to Sweden. We had never before discussed or suggested a move to Sweden but suddenly it was decided.

The timing was right. Both Jon and I were free. We had guest contracts in the opera houses where we were performing and could live wherever we wanted, as long as we were close to airports. The house in Sweden was only about an hour away from Copenhagen airport, or it was possible to take a ferry to Travemuende.

Of course, we also considered Jack. It would be beautiful for him too. The sea was just a hundred metres away and it was a wonderful neighbourhood, with lots of children for Jack to play with.

The house would be ours from 1 April 1976.

Chapter Five

Music is the soul's thoughts.
Leo Tolstoy

The move to Sweden, 1976

The move to Sweden was a big step, but strangely enough it didn't turn out to be as complicated or physically demanding as I had imagined. I had nightmares for weeks about packing and cleaning up the apartment. I was worried that I would forget something. Somehow it was all done and fixed without any great dramas. Well perhaps one.

I decided to paint the apartment while Jon was away for a couple of days in London, to make it look nice for the next occupants. It was tricky trying to stop Jack from joining in, but otherwise I thought I did a stunning job – that is, until Jon returned. Staring at the walls, absolutely dumbfounded, he asked in a trembling voice, 'Who is the idiot that has made such a mess of the apartment?' Before I had time to answer him, he followed up by wondering how on earth we could possibly get someone in to fix the disaster before we left for Sweden.

I'm happy to admit that this was my first but not my last attempt to show Jon that I am quite a good interior decorator.

The drive to Sweden on the first day of April was for me, an unbelievable feeling. Returning to my homeland with my family was a wonderful adventure. We were already familiar with the house, having stayed with Ingalill and Ralph many times.

After I unlocked the front door, Jon insisted on carrying me over the threshold. Jack demanded that he should also be introduced to our new home the same way. He was nearly two years old and a big boy, but not too big to be carried.

The furniture arrived that night. To make it easy and quick for everyone, we just had everything put in a big heap in one of the rooms. The two moving men had a couple of hours left before they had to be back on the ferry to Travemünde, and I decided to give them something that would make them remember Sweden. This unforgettable something was a Swedish delicacy called surstromming.

Surstomming is a dish of herrings that have been placed in barrels to ferment for a couple of months, and then put in tins. When you feel you cannot wait any longer for the feast, you take a tin and an opener, walk outside, and look for a place to sit, as far away as you can from other human beings. This is vitally important!

The smell – well, it's indescribable. There simply are no words in the world that could describe this deadly stink. But the taste of surstromming is delicious.

I have to admit I was a bit annoyed about the moving men's bad manners. They left without a single word.

First winter in Sweden, 1976

Chapter Six

Music washes away from the soul the dust of everyday life.
Berthold Auerbach

Life in Sweden

Living in our own place in beautiful Hollviken was wonderful. When Jon and I happened to be free and at home at the same time, it was heaven. However, living in Sweden didn't change our professional routine, which did add some extra pressure on us all, Jack included.

As a norm I would have two or three performance in Germany every week. This meant a lot of travelling, and when I look back I wonder how the three of us survived without collapsing under the lifestyle stress we were faced with.

I would normally have Jack with me at all performances. That was quite a lot of travelling for a little two-year-old boy. He didn't seem to mind though, and I had the feeling he actually enjoyed playing around at night in my dressing room. My dressers were beautiful women and didn't seem to mind having a little guy running around their feet.

There were times when it became too much. It happened not once, but many times, that I would find Jack in the middle of a performance, having a great time, hiding behind me on the stage together with the chorus. Somehow he had no trouble finding his way on to the stage, and the people in charge, didn't mind him sneaking out into the limelight.

Jon was now mainly performing the *Ring*. Added to the performances still running at the English National Opera in London and the opera house in Leipzig were two new productions in Dortmund and Geneva.

The premiere in Geneva was planned for June and, as I happened to have three days free, we decided that both Jack and I would fly down to Switzerland with Jon. A lovely lady in Kiel, who was extremely supportive of Jon and me in our professional lives, offered to come to Geneva to look after Jack. This meant I would be able to sit in on Jon's dress rehearsal. We were quite excited and looking forward to the whole event.

Jon had the misfortune to occasionally be affected by violent allergies. This would make his throat very sore and it was almost impossible for him to use his voice. The dress rehearsal in Geneva happened to be one of those unfortunate occasions. *Siegfried* in Wagner's Ring is not a role that a singer can just 'mark' (use half your volume). It is full on for five hours. Jon could not even talk. The opera house had not been able to find another tenor prepared to jump in and save the performance. As a solution, Jon went on stage, miming and acting Siegfried for five hours, while another tenor was standing in the pit singing the role.

I do not know how he did it. I would have thrown in the towel.

The next day Jon's voice was non-existent and sadly he informed the opera house that he was unable to perform that night. Luckily they found a tenor who was able to step in, and the Weavings were free to leave and fly back home.

Sweden can be heaven on earth but, just as easily the other way around depending on the weather. We Swedes are used to accepting one out of three summers turning out beautifully. When that happens we truly enjoy being alive and praise our luck for living in such a paradise.

Our first summer in Sweden turned out to be absolutely perfect! We also had about two months of free time on our hands, and this gave us the opportunity to really settle in our new home. Our daily routine consisted of hours by the sea and wonderful times by the barbecue with new friends and neighbours. Jon spent almost as much time on the golf courses as he did at home. Knowing that he was enjoying his new life at the North Pole made me very happy.

Midsummer is a special time for all Swedes and Jon and I were invited to perform in a television show for this yearly celebration.

The program was filmed in Karlstad, a city in the middle of Sweden, where my two boys had never been before. It was also the first time they participated in a traditional Midsummer Eve ceremony. This involved dancing around a midsummer pole with a wreath of flowers on your head. I am pleased to say I got a shot of my beautiful little son seconds before he chucked away the annoying flowers.

I remember performing in Karlstad some ten years earlier. One day I had stood on a bridge in the middle of the city. It was mid-January, snow everywhere, and the river was covered in thick ice. Out of the blue I felt spring in the air! A sudden puff of air had touched my face, the only uncovered part of my body, and without question, that puff told me spring was on its way. Totally unlikely, considering the snowy landscape in front of me, but these ten seconds are so vivid in my memory and will stay with me forever.

Jack at Midsummer, Sweden, 1978

Perhaps the first 'spring feeling' is something we mad Swedes are sensitive to.

For two years I had only been speaking German with Jack, but after moving to Sweden we had to change our conversation to Swedish. Jon and Jack communicated only in English. This enabled Jack to express himself in three different languages and he still can today.

Jon also taught Jack Australian humour and I am not sure if this was a good idea. I am reminded over and over again by friends about a cheeky little two-year-old's comment when asked 'Are you tired, Jack?' He replied, 'Yes, of you.'

When we discussed having children, Jon agreed to have a child if it did not lessen the love I had for him. As an only child, he could be selfish. Jon did not want to have only one child – if we were going to have children, he wanted three or four. He remembered the loneliness he had felt as a child. Sadly, due to the thrombosis I incurred after my surgery, I was advised not have any more children.

Jon loved Jack and was a good father, although rather old-fashioned and strict. I was the easygoing parent. On one occasion, Jon, Jack and a neighbour of ours were on their way by car from Malmö to Oslo to attend a performance I was giving at the opera house. On the way, they stopped at a cafe to have something to eat.

Jon asked Jack to go to get a waiter so they could order some coffee. Jack attracted a waiter's attention, and when he appeared, Jack informed him that 'two old buggers want coffee'. We treated Jack as a small adult rather than a child. He was always with us, wherever we went, and clearly had picked up quite a vocabulary!

I was engaged for a new production of *Das Feuerwerk* in the Bielefeld Opera House in Germany. Rehearsals were to start in late September. This meant I had to be away from home and my two boys for about four weeks, which wasn't something I was looking forward to. But it had to be done. While I was away, Jon's best friend in Australia, Keith, came to visit Jon in Sweden, which was perfect timing. The guys, Jack included of course, were free to do anything they liked.

Das Feuerwerk became well known in the 1950s after one of its main songs, *O, mein Papa* became a big hit all around the world. I had never been involved with this musical and didn't really know what to expect. As it turned out, I felt like the cat that stole the cream. It was as if the main role, Iduna, had been tailor-made for me. A heavenly feeling. I could really just be myself. Iduna is even expected to have an accent! The cast was fantastic and my colleague and male lead, Helmut Kegler, and his wife Christine, became very good friends and visited us later in Australia.

Das Feuerwerk, Bielefeld, 1975

One of Iduna's songs is dedicated to a horse and I was to be introduced to my animal friend at the last dress rehearsal. I had been asking for days about the horse. How big was it? What colour was it? It was the first time I had performed with a four-legged animal and I was quite excited, even though I had heard the saying, 'Never perform with children or animals.' After this occasion, I understood exactly why.

The opera house was packed as usual with invited guests for the dress rehearsal. My introduction to my four-legged colleague did not happen until two minutes before we were to enter the stage together. I was in shock. The horse was HUGE! The music started and there was no time to hesitate. I pulled the horse behind me on to the stage. For a couple of seconds everything went as planned. While singing, I walked around the stage with the horse held safely by the reins.

We went along nicely for a couple of seconds. What happened next is something that no one in the theatre that night, will ever forget. The horse decided to show the audience who was the real star that night and the positions changed. He began to race around the stage in circles with me hanging on to the reins for dear life, my singing becoming a scream. It felt like a year had passed before some brave stage- hands managed to control the horse and rescue me.

Surprisingly, the people in charge of the opera house were actually somewhat pleased about the incident. They had been terrified the horse was going to fall into the orchestra pit and that would have been a total disaster. You won't be surprised when I tell you there was no horse on stage on opening night. Instead of singing to a four-legged friend, I was now provided with four ballet girls sitting around me with horse masks on their heads. Not very believable but at least it was safe!

Jon, Jack and Keith had come to the dress rehearsal and had told me how the horse incident had affected and scared the audience. It certainly did not affect one member of the audience – Jack. As a child, he loved being with and on horses.

Jack and I celebrated New Year's Eve, 1976 by ourselves in Hollviken with our neighbours. Jon had a performance in London, and Jack and I picked him up at the airport in Hannover a week later on our way to one of my performances in the New Year in Bielefeld. When we returned to Sweden the following day, I received a lovely message from Storan, Gothenburg, offering me guest performances in *The Gypsy Princess* in April.

Yeaaaah! Gothenburg, here I come.

The opera house in Kiel had heard about the successful production of *Das Feuerwerk* in Bielefeld and wanted me for their new production of the same musical the following autumn. They promised there would be no horses involved so I grabbed the opportunity.

It had been quite a while since Jon and I performed together in the same production and we were delighted to be offered the two leading parts in a production of Paul Lincke's *Frau Luna* in Basel, Switzerland. However, there was one small problem. The timetables for *Das Feuerwerk* in Kiel and *Frau Luna* were almost identical. I managed to make arrangements with the two opera houses regarding the rehearsals which enabled us to go ahead with both productions. In the meantime I had to fit *The Merry Widow* in Munich and *Das Feuerwerk* in Bielefeld into my schedule. Jon of course had his performances in London, Manchester and Leipzig. Somehow, unbelievable as it seemed, we believed we could work it out. Would I consider something like that today? Forget it! We must have been crazy.

What would Jack's opinion have been, if we had asked him, I wonder? Our little son spoke three languages from the cradle, and travelled all over Europe before he was three years old. Some would think him very lucky, but in the process he had often to wave one or the other of his parents goodbye, sometimes for weeks at a time.

In between everything, we did television shows occasionally in Germany and Sweden. Most of the time, this was fun. I remember filming a duet with John van Kesteren. I was supposed to drink a glass of champagne during the singing. In the theatre it is rare to get the real thing when drinking or eating are called for. I was more than a bit surprised, but pleased, when I took the first sip and realized it was real champagne. The filming took seven 'takes' and if the people in charge had known it would take this many, they would more wisely have given me mineral water. During the last 'take' I did not have to pretend I was tipsy. I actually had to concentrate really hard on trying *not* to look tipsy. That was hard work.

During a live Easter show on Swedish television, Jon was taken backstage and without the knowledge of the host, Lasse Holmquist, got dressed up as a Swedish 'Pask Karring' (an old woman with a broomstick). Lasse was completely confused by his unknown guest who suddenly appeared. I hardly recognized Jon myself. It was live television and the show had to go on despite the surprise. Many of my Swedish friends who had never met Jon later expressed their concerns regarding my choice of a husband.

During the filming of a television program in Malmo we formed a friendship with Gunilla Marcus, whose American husband Norman was visiting her. We invited them home to Hollviken for dinner one night. Jon and Norman got on really well as both were deeply interested in music. Jon, believing Norman to be an amateur, was impressed with his knowledge about music. When it was time to leave, Jon asked Norman for his surname. 'Luboff' was the reply. Jon was utterly speechless and overcome with embarrassment. This was a rare occurrence for Jon. I had heard the name but knew little about American choirs. Jon had a sleepless night. During his time as a young announcer at the ABC in Melbourne, he had almost daily been playing records of the world famous Norman Luboff Choir. He could not believe he had assumed Norman was a total music amateur and treated him as such for the whole evening. Norman, on the other hand, had enjoyed his night of anonymity.

Stora Teatern in Gothenburg had been my artistic home during my four years with Alice and Styrbjörn Lindedal in the 1950s. Not a day passed without a discussion of what was happening in the theatre, rehearsals, planning new productions or dealing with cancellations. Persuading Gothenburg to understand and support the building of a new opera house became one of Styrbjörn's bigger tasks. After twenty years of frustration and discussions he at last had his dream realized. I am sure there was a very happy Styrbjörn smiling in heaven on the day the new opera house was finished and opened its doors.

Monique and Jon, Show Boat, Augsburg, 1972

To be performing on the stage of Stora Teatern for the very first time meant a lot to me and was something I had been dreaming about since I was introduced to this beautiful place twenty years earlier.

I was very familiar with *The Gypsy Princess* as I had already performed in a couple of productions in Germany. I just had to change into Swedish. One of my oldest friends, Claes Jacobsson, was also in the cast, and this made it even more exciting. We had done many concerts together but had never performed in the same production.

The feeling I experienced when out on the stage in front of the full house is difficult to describe. Many times I have tried unsuccessfully to explain how it felt. The air was 'thick', as if I could actually grab it in my hands. It felt as if there was electricity in the air. There was a quietness you could 'hear'. I discovered later that it was not just my imagination. Colleagues, even people from the orchestra, came into my dressing room afterwards, and told me that they had never experienced anything like it before.

I know there were people in the audience who had been part of my life in many different ways. There were old school friends, teachers, neighbours, family friends, relatives and people who felt they wanted to catch up with me and see me as a performer. The energy I picked up from the public created the performance. This experience is what we artists dream and pray will happen during every performance but of course it doesn't. When it does, it's magic.

People from the opera house in Oslo, Norway, saw the performance and decided to acquire the production and put it in their repertoire the following year, 1978. The new Intendant at Stora Teatern, Folke Abenius, knew Jon, having directed him in operas in Germany. He asked if I would be interested in taking part in the Norwegian production. I thought it could be fun, so I accepted. I had never sung in Oslo before. All I had to do was learn the part in Norwegian. I did not think it would be a problem.

Music and Love

Monique dressed for *The Gypsy Princess*, Gothenburg, 1977

During the summer holidays, Jack and I flew to London, to join Jon, who as usual was busy with the *Ring*. During a break between performances we drove up north and stayed in a very old and isolated house in the Lake District. There was no other house in sight, and a couple of hours after the sun had gone down, I experienced what real darkness is all about.

I remember standing in the bedroom with Jack on the first floor. Jack, for some reason, had turned off the light. I knew he was there because I could hear him talking. But I could not see him or anything else. It was uncanny. This was not just darkness. It was as if I was

Jon and Jack, England, 1977

totally blind. I found myself feeling slightly hysterical before the light was turned on again. How did people manage years ago without electricity? One takes so many things for granted and we don't always appreciate what we have until it's not there anymore.

The tenth of August was the date the fun started – rehearsals in Basel. This meant seven weeks of total stress for Jon who had to travel almost every second day between London and Basel. He did it!

It was an easy task for me until 19 September, when I was expected to be in Kiel for the last two weeks of the rehearsals for *Das Feuerwerk*. Somehow I managed to be in two places at the same time between 19 and 25 September for the first night of *Luna* in Basel. Probably because of the stress, I don't have much memory of the

Luna performances except that it was great to be together again with Jon on stage.

There was one incident that happened during the rehearsals in Basel that I think is worth mentioning. As we all know, Switzerland is like Sweden, a neutral and safe country.

We had engaged a young woman from Sweden to come with us and look after Jack, at the times when we were both rehearsing. One weekend Jon had to fly to London and I had to go to Munich for a performance. I took Jack with me so that our babysitter could have the time off to relax and just enjoy herself.

When Jack and I got back from Munich, the apartment was empty. The baby sitter was gone! Later in the day there was a phone call from a hospital, asking us to come to pick her up. She had been attacked in the middle of the city of Basel. Two men had tried to force her into their car. She screamed and luckily people came to her assistance and brought her to the hospital, where she had been kept overnight because of her injuries.

The hospital staff called the police to report what had happened. They were stunned by the police response – 'Such things don't happen in Basel'. That was it!

Together with the administrative people in Kiel, we worked out a timetable to suit us all. This meant they rehearsed without me for the first three weeks, and I attended the two last weeks before the first night. It worked out well for us all and I enjoyed stepping into my comfortable role as Iduna again.

Being in four different productions made the rest of 1977 rather busy. But I did it! Jack, of course, was sharing all these events with us. One day, Jack and I were having something to eat at a small eatery in Kiel before one of my performances. A couple asked if they could share the table with us, and of course that was quite all right.

Jack had a children's picture book (one that taught counting) that a friend of ours had given him. He was bored stiff by it, but opened it on the request of the couple. They looked and listened with interest to Jack explaining how 2 apples + 1 apple becomes 3 apples etc.

After a couple of minutes, Jack turned to me, his hand hiding his mouth, and whispered, 'Old people!'

Jon was contracted to film a newly written opera for the ABC in Australia, and flew to Melbourne at the end of November. He promised to be back home in time for Christmas.

Our Christmas turned out to be very special as my mother Greta, was staying with us. Greta became a true inspiration to us all. Despite her disabilities – unable to talk or move the left side of her body – she hardly ever showed any sadness or distress during the seventeen years she was anchored to her wheelchair.

January brought lots of snow to Hollviken and we cuddled up as much as we could inside our cosy little home. It didn't happen as often as we would have liked because we had a full quota of performances. Travelling in snowstorms unfortunately forced us once or twice to have to notify opera houses that we wouldn't be able to turn up to certain performances due to flights or ferries being cancelled. That did not make us popular.

At the end of January, I had a phone call from Kalle Kinch, director of Folkan Theatre in Stockholm. He was planning a new production of *A Little Night Music* with amongst others, Zarah Leander and my friend Claes Jacobsson, in the cast. The rehearsals would start in September. Would I be interested in taking part? I gave them a 'Yes' after discussing it with Jon. I personally was quite excited about the thought of being back on the stage in Stockholm. I hoped that it could also lead to more engagements in my home country and cutting down on the constant travelling abroad.

A couple of days later, I had a desperate phone call from my agent in Munich. 'Das Operettenhaus', a theatre in Hamburg where mainly musicals were shown, had just been sold, and the new owners were planning to pull it down and build a new theatre complex. To get some extra income before the building was demolished they had

The Gypsy Princess, Oslo, 1978

decided to put on *Land of Smiles* for a couple of weeks. They put aside two days for rehearsals. TWO! Even if you have no stage experience yourself, I am sure you would be shaking your head when reading this. But that was the situation. Harry Schmidt got together singers, each one already familiar with one specific role, a splendid director, conductor and orchestra and, believe it or not, after two days' rehearsals we delivered a very successful *Land of Smiles*. Admittedly we did the performance without a chorus, and we all brought our own costumes. It just shows what one can do under pressure.

Sadly it reminded me that the last time I sang the role of Lisa, the lead in this operetta, was the unforgettable night during the Olympics when it was decided in thirty minutes to change from *The Merry Widow* to *Land of Smiles*. Clearly a remarkably useful operetta.

Chapter Seven

Life is a lot like jazz...it's best when you improvise.
George Gershwin

The deciding moment!

On 25 February, Jon was on his way from Berlin to Cape Town. He had forgotten to bring lighter clothing with him and asked me to bring what he needed and meet him at Hamburg airport. He had one hour on his hands between changing planes. It was not difficult for me as I was driving to Hamburg anyway, to appear in *Land of Smiles*.

Jack and I arrived at the airport to find that Jon's plane was about thirty minutes late. When he disembarked from one plane he had to run, and I mean *run*, with us behind him, to the terminal for the South African departure gate. Standing in the Cape Town queue, he grabbed the bag I was holding, pulled out a pair of trousers and proceeded to strip off the ones he was wearing.

Jack and I, and the people around us in the queue, stared as Jon began to put on the fresh trousers. In a slightly hysterical voice he attempted to explain to the people around him that a stewardess had spilt coffee on his clothes. He stopped, took a big breath and declared, 'This is it! What are we doing? We can't live like this!'

And that was it! That was the unplanned, deciding moment when we knew we had to change our lives. Stress had taken over not just our professional lives but also our private family life.

The circumstances of Jon's decision meant that it was not the time for us to sit down and begin a conversation about what should happen next. Catching the flight was the priority. We kissed and parted with the unspoken understanding that we would deal with the situation as soon as Jon was back from Cape Town the following week. When Jon returned, it did not take us long to make up our minds about what we were going to do.

Jon felt he had reached his goal when he was signed up for the whole *Ring* cycle at the English National Opera and Leipzig opera house in the 1970s. To perform both Siegmund and Siegfried was a dream come true for a Wagnerian tenor. Jon sang both roles from 1974 until 1978. I don't think there are many Wagnerian tenors who have sung the *Ring* in both English and German at the same time. I remember Jon coming home after a performance and telling me he had found himself mixing English and German in the middle of an aria. He was hoping no one noticed.

He was happy and satisfied with his life and felt it was time to relax. We both felt we had completed our stage work in Europe. Jon wanted to play golf, catch up with old friends and have more time with Jack and me. We wanted to find avenues that did not demand constant travel and separation. We decided that to have a liveable future we would move to Australia. The decision was made.

I had been to Australia and I loved it. I knew it would be a wonderful place for Jack to grow up.

Jon's mother was getting older and he wanted to spend more time with her. He had been in Europe for twenty years. The hard thing for me was leaving my mother, even though I knew my sister and brother would be close by. I would miss all three of them.

I said goodbye to my mentors Styrbjörn and Alice. These two wonderful people gave me boundless love and support as well as nurturing my career. They had no children and I believe gave me the love they would have given their own children. I am so lucky to have met Alice in the local store on that day so many years ago.

Alice and Styrbjörn Lindedal with Jon and Monique,
Sweden, 1969

Styrbjörn Lindedal was First Conductor at Stora Teatern in Gothenburg for thirty years, from 1938 to 1968 and later Director from 1970 to 1971. He died on 5 May 1991after a dramatic accident.

He was leaving from their first-floor apartment for a rehearsal at the theatre. As Alice waved goodbye, he stumbled, fell down the stairs and died. It was thought he may have had a heart attack. After witnessing the tragedy, Alice never recovered. She fell into a deep depression and was admitted into psychiatric care where she remained until her death three years later.

The last time I saw them was on 28 April 1990. Jon and I flew to Gothenburg to celebrate my fiftieth birthday with a show I named 'Monica's Kalas' (Monica's Celebration). I did not expect a big audience as I hadn't been in Sweden for a long time, but the show was sold out and so I performed it again next day. Alice and Styrbjörn came to the show and we had a lovely reunion afterwards. It has been a wonderful memory to hold of those two dear people.

We needed to begin dealing with our commitments with all the different opera companies. This was not altogether easy. I was to appear in the new production of *The Gypsy Princess* coming up in Oslo and the last performance was scheduled for mid-June, so there was no problem there. After private talks with the people in charge of the German opera houses, a friendly decision was reached. It was agreed that we would keep in constant contact and notify them if we planned to return to Europe.

Folkan Theatre in Stockholm accepted the cancellation of my appearance in *A Little Night Music.*

It was very emotional for both of us to say 'auf wiedersehen' to colleagues and productions, but we knew we could return if the move to Australia did not work out.

We made an appointment for Jack and me with the Australian embassy in Copenhagen. I was a little nervous, fearing they may have insisted I had a steady and reliable income, but they were not interested in me. They took longer processing Jack as they wanted to ensure he had no disabilities or illnesses. After a short time we received the green light.

We were ready to go.

I did not ever hear Jon utter one word about missing being on stage after we left Europe.

I am thankful for the time and place I have been given on earth.
        Good moments – blessed embraces.
        Bad moments – lectures for the soul.

Finale

Thanks to Jon, I was fortunate enough to have the opportunity to acquire a second homeland on the other side of the world – Australia! I have *never* met anyone who's been visiting this wonderful part of the world who hasn't absolutely adored it here.

Monique as Adele in *Die Fledermaus*, Sydney, 1982

Finale

The Weavings moved 'down under' to give their only son, Jack, the opportunity to grow up in paradise – plenty of space, great weather, great beaches, friendly and easygoing people, lots of different cultures, and family connections.

Jack settled easily into the Australian way of life. He took to the water like a fish; even today, he is out there daily (or as often as he can be) on his surfboard, introducing his young son Björn to the heaven of surfing.

Jon and I had more or less resigned from the stage and decided we would live like an ordinary family at last. Well, that was our plan. But people soon got to know we were back. The ABC was the first to offer us work, sending us on tour all over Australia, which, to be honest, was fun! We were performing together *and* had Jack with us. It had all worked out just as we had planned; even better, in fact.

There were of course also TV concerts and televised operetta productions from the Sydney Opera House. The best New Year's Eve concerts I've ever done were the seven in a row (from 1985 to 1992) in the Sydney Opera House. That was magic. In between we also managed to run a theatre restaurant, open a clog factory, and start the Academy of Singing, a singing school that is still running with great success in Melbourne. Annika Tregonning, one of the sweetest and most talented of the young singers who I taught some twenty years ago, is now the successful head teacher of the Academy of Singing.

In 2011, Jon and I decided to make a bold move and breathe some European air again. We moved to Sweden. Sadly Jon passed away suddenly just six months after we had established our new home, which was a dreadful shock.

Somehow I felt as if my life had stopped.

The loving support of my friends and family helped me through the difficult days, weeks, months – even years – after Jon's death. Singing and performing have also eased the loss. Life is again busy and meaningful: always planning ahead, concerts, recordings, being a mother and a grandmother, enjoying warm and wonderful relationships with friends and colleagues. I have so much to be thankful for, all the joys, experiences, successes, and I wake up in the morning without pain!

It has all been a wonderful blessing. And it still is.

Nicholas Braithwaite (left), Richard Bonynge (centre) and Jon, Melbourne, 2008

Jon at the piano on New Year's Eve, Melbourne, 2010

Acknowledgements

My first and greatest debt and gratitude is owed to Alice and Styrbjörn Lindedal, my musical and personal mentors, and substitute godparents, for their love and exceptional support during my musical development. My mother Greta, who let me step out into the world of music. My sister, Rosa, and her beautiful family, who unfailingly always been by my side offering support and encouragement.

My husband Jon, during our forty years together, encouraged me to continue my career, even though it meant many periods of separation. We worked separately, and together, in demanding roles in many locations, and his steadfast enthusiasm for my career was a constant blessing.

With the support of Erland Hagegård, professionally and privately, I have started singing again later in life. His presence and helpful comments have been invaluable in the last couple of years.

I have been unbelievably lucky to find wonderful friends, both on stage and in private life, all over the world. I am concerned that if I begin mentioning names, I might forget someone and cause hurt. You, dear friends, know how important your friendship has been to me and how grateful I am to be in your friendship circle.

I have taught some amazing young people. One of these talented singers is Annika Tregonning, who not only has become one of my closest friends, but also is now the Head teacher and director of Academy of Singing in Melbourne. Through her, Jon's and my singing lives on.

My friend Gillian Nikakis has created much of this book from my very raw material. It would never have become a book without her tireless work. To her I offer boundless thanks and much love.

My dear son Jack's beautiful wife, Nicole, has supported and helped me in many different ways, psychologically and practically. She is good with words and intelligent and kind, and I thank her for all that she has done for me.

My boy, Jack Björn Weymouth Weaving – now a man with a beautiful son of his own – has encouraged me in the work of writing, as he always supported the things I do.

Thank you, Jack, - you are the most important person among all those who I love.

Singing technique

Music is a moral law. It gives soul to the universe, wings to the mind, flight to the imagination, and charm and gaiety to life and everything.
Plato

The singing technique that I have developed over many years as a professional singer, and that I still use, is based on traditional bel canto techniques. The technique rests on how we were born to use our voices, a natural process that is easy to understand even for a young child because of its simplicity.

I am very inspired by the positive responses I have had from singers and students when using this technique. This is truly a technique that can be used by singers of all genres of music.

Love what you do

I have always loved what I've been doing, and to love what you do is a gift that I would like everyone to have. Pleasure, interest, enjoyment and total commitment to something gives us confidence and thus the greatest opportunity for success.

Singing is natural, just like speaking: singing is sustained speech. Babies often make singing noises before they learn how to speak. Singing needs to be free and natural for you to be able to express inner feelings through your voice.

When you speak, your voice changes 'colour' depending on the emotion you are feeling, and when you sing it should be the same.

Everyone who has a normal speaking voice is able to sing, which we all do in situations where we feel relaxed and comfortable – for instance in the shower, driving alone, or in a large crowd.

The physical and psychological benefits from singing are many. People often describe a feeling of well-being after singing. Here is a list of common benefits of singing.

- Exercises the lungs, tones up the intercostal muscles and the diaphragm
- Benefits the heart and circulation by improving aerobic capacity
- Decreases muscle tension
- Opens up sinuses and respiratory tubes for improved breathing
- Tones facial muscles and improves posture
- Releases pain-relieving endorphins
- Increases self-esteem and confidence, reduces anxiety and stress.

Feeling good after singing is a natural effect of the release of endorphins, and from making beautiful sounds!

Classical singers

Most of my singing students have asked me the following question at some time during their studies: 'Do you think I'll make it?' My answer is always, 'I don't know. You have everything you need to succeed – great talent, good technique, repertoire that suits you, an interesting personality etc. If you are one of the lucky ones who happen to be at the right place at the right time – yes, then you've got the chance to make it. If you keep on being focused and committed, then I believe you will make it.'

Apart from luck, to succeed you will need:

Talent
Education – the more the better

Dedication – the more the better
Experience – the more the better

Finding your true voice

1. The physical warm-up

Drop forward/down from waist and slowly 'roll up' – head last.
End up straight, not tense.

2. The psychological warm-up

Step into a blissfully happy mood. (Suggestion: See yourself putting bags of personal stressful things/thoughts into an air balloon and, when it's full, let it fly away up into the sky. You'll feel free and can walk/dance away.)

3. The voice warm-up

Take a deep breath.
Release the air with a sigh of blissful happiness – 'aaaaah'.

Basic singing technique

1. Breath control

Relearning natural breathing.
Breathing = emotion = energy.

2. Posture

Pinocchio posture.
Imagine hanging on a string. The spine is straight – not stiff.

3. Surprise lift (soft palate)

Yawning *without* tension.

4. Speaking – singing

Singing is sustained speech.
Speaking technique needs to be 'healthy'.

5. **Resonance**

Learn how to use the body as a loudspeaker (chest, 'mask', head etc.).

6. **Warm-up exercises**

Rrrrrrr, mmmmm, sighing.

i-aaaaa–arpeggio or quick scales.

One of the most powerful techniques I learnt from my first teacher Alice Lindedal was to sing on the vowel 'ö'. It helps project the voice forward while keeping everything open and free at the back of the mouth.

Dare to sing

The magic word is 'preparation'.

Work on your voice on a daily basis (except when tired or sick). There are no short- cuts.

Singing is a sport and requires training.

Speak the lyrics before you sing them.

Try to find natural physical expressions (hands, facial expression, posture).

What you are saying/singing should be universally comprehensible. An audience of any nationality should be able to understand a good part of what you're saying just by looking at you and hearing the dynamics of your voice.

Choose a repertoire that is believable for your age and personality.

Never sing anything that is too hard for you.

In the theatre the eyes can fool the ears and steal the show.

And, most importantly: Be yourself – find your uniqueness!

Fear, stage fright and too much hubris

Fear can affect us both physically and psychologically. When confidence is restored, the singer is able to relax and use the natural supporting muscles of the voice, allowing air and sound to flow and resonate freely.

Most of us are shy, which stops us from allowing ourselves to 'let go'. This is something that we must confront and overcome before we will be able to be the person we are, in front of an audience. Great artists are all nervous in the moments before they enter the stage. This is a sign of emotional sensitivity. So – paradoxically – we should be thankful for the butterflies in the stomach before a performance. It indicates amongst other things that the energy/adrenaline necessary for performance is present.

Stage fright, also called performance anxiety, is an extreme version of the normal tension and heightened awareness that all performers feel before going on. True performance anxiety (which can bring increased blood pressure, sweating, a dry mouth, trembling and faster breathing) is very negative for singers.

Once again, practice is an essential ingredient in overcoming fear. Focusing and putting time aside to work on how to change negative habits and patterns will help to get rid of inhibitions. If the technique and subject details have been worked on and mastered, then a remaining nervousness can be due to not enough self-knowledge, or too much focus on 'self'.

Too much confidence can stem from a person believing he/she is better than and superior to everybody else. The ability to show a true or genuine personality without fear has nothing to do with egotism.

Here are some ideas on how to deal with and overcome fear or stage fright.

1. **Physical approach**

When nervous or tense, stand up and let your stomach 'drop – not your posture, just the stomach. This makes it possible for the diaphragm muscle to move downwards which allows the lungs to expand and fill up with air.

Be aware of the tension and the tightness in your stomach disappearing, making it possible for you to take deep breaths. Fear creates the tendency to stop breathing, or breathe erratically, and results in too little oxygen and too much carbon monoxide in the bloodstream. Naturally, this causes the feeling of fear to increase.

Take charge of your breathing and begin to release the tension. Slow down and concentrate only on your breathing. Continue until you can feel that your breathing has returned to a normal rhythm, and your stomach muscles are being released at every intake of air.

2. Psychological approach

Fear exists in our imagination.

We all know that if we say 'I can', then the possibility for success is there. We are also aware that people who don't believe in themselves seldom succeed.

Accept fear for what it is – a state of mind. As a rule we are afraid of the unknown, so take a pen and paper, search your mind and write down the reasons for your fears. If you examine carefully each reason you have written down, and think logically about whether they are realistic fears, your fear will diminish.

3. Practical approach

Performing is a job. To make it look easy you must work hard.

The more time you put into the studying the technique and refining the interpretation, the more comfortable and confident you will feel. Experience also helps to lessen the fear. As you gain more experience, the fear will lessen. Overcoming an excess of fear will give you the freedom to find your own stage personality and let your charisma shine. Allow yourself to enjoy what you are doing and the audience will appreciate what you are giving them.

Select recordings

Many recordings of Jon and Monique singing, separately and together, can be found on YouTube. Here is a list of some of Monique's favourites.

Monique:

'Schwipslied', https://www.youtube.com/watch?v=7jZfJnKc2H8

'Schwipslied', www.youtube.com/watch?v=276LU330pFk

'O mein Papa', www.youtube.com/watch?v=IsO-bmt6ML4

'Mein Herr Marquis', https://www.youtube.com/watch?v=4ocGud3d-Rc

Monique and Jon together:

'Am Manzanares', https://www.youtube.com/watch?v=fmrwcooPFd0

Music for the People concert, www.youtube.com/watch?v=-b43K3Yh_dg

Jon:

'In fernem Land', https://www.youtube.com/watch?v=ZLCC0SZpfYw

'Song from Vienna', https://www.youtube.com/watch?v=mM2_SAiF7iQ

'Strangers in Paradise', www.youtube.com/watch?v=5tpydeLmRK0

'Song from Lilac Time', www.youtube.com/watch?v=ImymMywqAsY

Select recordings

More information about Monique and Jon and links to other recordings can be found on the following websites:

www.academyofsinging.com

www.singinglessons.com.au

www.moniquebrynnel.com

Index

The index contains only persons mentioned in the text.

Abenius, Folke, 219
Adami, Mme Poppy, 24
Aitken, Eric, 24, 26, 27
Alexander, Dr Alfred, 146, 188
Allman, Robert, 54
Amble-Naess, Lief, 112
Ashcroft, Dame Peggy, 37
Asmundsen, Sven, 93
Åstrand, Mona, 125

Bailey, Norman, 63
Beresford, Hugh, 57
Bindley, Pauline, 24
Björling, Renée, 105
Blair, Eva, 12
Blee, Norman, 19
Bonynge, Richard, xiii, 35, 55, 232
Borgioli, Dino, 23, 26, 43
Boughton, Rutland, 28
Braithwaite, Nicholas, 189, 190, 232
Brandt, Bernhard, 74
Brandt, Bernhardina, 75-6
Brandt, Bertholdy, 75
Brandt, Greta Viola, 74, 76, 81, 148, 198-9, 223
Brandtska Solist Familjen, 74, 75
Bronhill, June, xiii, 27, 37, 45, 47, 48
Brownlee, John, 23

Brynnel, Erik, 78-9, 163-4, 166
Brynnel, Lasse, 79, 80
Brynnel, Rose Marie, 79, 80, 98, 148, 163, 166, 189, 202

Callas, Maria, 13
Calve, Emma, 23
Carr, Keith, 213, 215
Charlesworth, Gil, 15
Clements, John, 12
Coates, Edith, 55
Coleman, Eric, 20
Coleman, Ronald, 20
Collier, Marie, xiii
Copley, John, 35, 36
Corelli, Franco, 155
Craig, Charles, 40
Crawford, Hector, 24
Crowfoot, Alan, 48
Cullberg, Bo, 84, 88

Dal Monte, Toti, 43
Darnley, John, 32
Dawson, Peter, 26
Dellert, Kjerstin, 106
Dowd, Ronald, xiii, 41
Dowling, Dennis, 42
Dunn, Geoffrey, 47

Index

Ebner, Josef, 129
Eckert, Karl, 135
Elkins, Margreta, xiii
Ellis, Norman, 16

Falk, Lauritz, 95
Fechner, Mr, 181
Folley, Lawrence, 41
Forsell, Harriet, 95, 96
Fretwell, Elizabeth, xiii, 41

Gester, Stan, 112
Gilly, Dingh, 23
Goodall, Reginald, 197
Grybe, Stig, 105
Gyse, Ingalill and Ralph, 207, 209

Hagegård, Erland, 171
Hambley, Eric, 21
Hammond, Joan, xiii
Hancock, Len, 58
Hansson, Albin, 77
Heddle Nash, John, 56
Hemmings, Peter, 36
Heussermann, Johann Christoph, 74
Hirsch, Heinrich, 160-1
Hobson, Valerie, 25
Hoffman, Peter, 67
Holmquist, Lasse, 217
Holmsten, Karl-Arne, 125
Horeton, Tom, 20
Howard, Patricia, xiii, 24
Howitt, Barbara, 41, 42
Hunter, Rita, 32, 55, 56, 57, 59-60
Hyland, Lennart, 85

Ingram, Lance, 13

Jacobsson, Claes, 219, 223
Johnson, James, 35

Kegler, Christine, 214
Kegler, Helmut, 214
Ken Lains' Orchestra, 86
Kennedy, Graham, 16, 19-20
Kinch, Kalle, 223
Koltai, Ralph, 63
Kulle, Jarl, 95, 96

Laane, Helga, 118, 119-20, 121, 122
Lagström, Solweig, 125
Lains, Ken, 85; orchestra, 86
Lane, Gloria, 44
Langford, Audrey, 71-2
Larsson, Egon, 104, 125
Lascelles, George Henry Hubert (7th Earl of Harewood), 58-9
Lawrence, Martin, 23
Leander, Zarah, 223
Lindedal, Styrbjörn, 87, 88, 91, 95, 96, 98, 100-1, 113, 130, 139, 142, 148, 217-18, 226-8
Lindquist, Ulf, 112
Lom, Herbert, 25
Lorenz, Max, 57
Luboff, Norman, 217

Mackerras, Sir Charles, 49, 57, 58, 197
Marchesi, Mathilde, 23
Marcus, Gunilla, 217
Martinsson, Harry, 76
Maxian, Fred, 166
McBeath, Kevin, 20
McMahon, Johnny, 16
Melba, Dame Nellie, 11, 23, 176
Menzies, Ivan, 12
Midgely, Walter, 43
Miller, Kevin, xiii, 48, 50, 51, 55
Modesti, Domenic, 14, 57
Moncrieff, Gladys, 12
Moore, Grace, 10

Morrow, Doretta, 28
Mort, Patricia, 24
Mummery, Browning, xiii, 26
Murray, Fred. 12

Neate, Ken, xiii, 58, 171-2
Nicholls, Cliff, 17
Nielson, Carrie, 126
Nilsson, Birgit, 58, 59
Nisbett, Margaret, xiii, 23, 48, 56
Norton, Geoff, 19, 20
Nygren, Rutger, 111, 114

Oldaker, Max, 12

Porter, Andrew, xiv
Powell Lloyd, Harry, 55
Powell, Brychan, 35
Pride, Malcolm, 47
Pscherer, Dr Kurt, 127, 150, 154

Quilico, Louis, 44

Rasin, Nils, 86
Raymond, Glenda, xiii, 24
Reid, Henry, 165
Reid, John, 36
Reid, Marcia, 165
Remedios, Alberto, 59
Riddell, Ruby, 12
Robinson, Dr, 188, 191
Rohling, Annie, 138, 158
Rosenthal, Harold, 20
Rysanek, Leonie, 63

Sandström, Roland, 112
Sartariano, Joseph, 56
Schmidt, Gertie, 138-9
Schmidt, Harry, 54, 224
Schmidt, Jessey, 13, 14
Schock, Rudolph, 44

Schuhmacher, Dr, 181, 182
Schulz, Robert, 54
Sharpe, Frederick, 48
Shaw, John, 41
Shaw, John, xiii
Shilling, Eric, 49, 50, 51
Skaug, Erna, 111
Skilondz, Madame, 108
Snell, Tiny, 15
Söderman, Ingalill, 113
Stabile, Mariano, 23
Steele, Suzanne, 36, 48, 54
Sterner, Alice, 87, 88, 91, 95, 96, 97, 98, 108, 113, 130, 139, 142, 148, 217, 226-8
Stroud, Geoffrey, 12
Sutherland, Dame Joan, xiii, 23, 35, 58, 88-9
Svensson, Jeanette, 94, 103-4
Svensson, Kirsten, 98
Swift, Tom, 28, 30-1

Tajnsek, Elisabeth, 183, 185
Tauber, Richard, 40, 45
Thelwell, Arthur, 29
Toye, Wendy, xiii, 46
Tregonning, Annika, 231
Tregonning, Jim, 20
Triguez, Madame Billy, 71, 98-100, 102
Tucker, Norman, 31, 36
Turner, Maggie, 182
Tutin, Dorothy, 37

van Kesteren, John, 216
Volker, Franz, 58-9
Vollardt, Gertrude, 172

Wand, Uwe, 204-5
Warren, Leonard, 54, 57
Weaving, Björn, 231

Weaving, Jack, 191, 195-6, 197,
    200, 203, 204-5, 209, 210-11,
    212, 216, 219-20, 222-3
Weaving, Marg, 166-7, 206-7
Weir, Beverley, 27
Weir, Len, 27
Westerberg, Bernd, 125

Zednik, Heinz, 126